Roger Basler de Roca

Prompted Minds

Prompted Minds

Cognition, Offloading and the Illusion of AI Understanding - or How Context, Bias and Models Shape the Future of Thinking

Roger Basler de Roca

Bibliographic information published by the Deutsche Nationalbibliothek: The Deutsche Nationalbibliothek lists this publication in the Deutsche Nationalbibliografie; detailed bibliographic data are available on the Internet at http://dnb.dnb.de.

Publisher: BoD · Books on Demand GmbH, Überseering 33, 22297 Hamburg, bod@bod.de

Printed by: Libri Plureos GmbH, Friedensallee 273, 22763 Hamburg

ISBN: 978-3-6957-4496-1

MIX
Papier aus verantwortungsvollen Quellen
Paper from responsible sources
FSC® C105338
www.fsc.org

Table of Contents

Prologue: The Question That Started Everything

It began with a simple question that I couldn't answer.

I was sitting in my office on a Tuesday morning in early 2024, wrestling with a complex research problem about cognitive offloading in decision-making systems. After hours of fruitless analysis, I turned to an AI assistant for help. Within seconds, it provided a comprehensive response that seemed to demonstrate deep understanding of the nuances involved. The analysis was sophisticated, well-structured, and appeared to grasp subtleties that had eluded me for hours.

But something felt wrong.

As I read through the AI's response, a nagging question emerged: Did this system actually understand what it was telling me, or was I witnessing an elaborate performance of understanding? The response was undeniably helpful, but was it genuine comprehension or a sophisticated illusion created by statistical pattern matching and computational processing?

This question haunted me because it revealed something profound about the moment we're living through. We are the first generation in human history to routinely interact with systems that can simulate understanding so convincingly that we often forget they might not actually understand anything at all. We ask questions and receive answers that seem to demonstrate intelligence, insight, and even wisdom. Yet beneath this compelling surface lies a fundamental uncertainty about the nature of machine cognition and its relationship to human understanding.

The more I explored this question, the more I realized it was just the beginning of a much larger inquiry. If AI systems can create such convincing illusions of understanding, what does this mean for human cognition? How are these interactions changing the way we think, learn, and know? What happens to human intelligence when we increasingly rely on artificial systems that may not truly understand the information they provide?

These questions led me on a journey of discovery that forms the foundation of this book. I found myself exploring research in neuroscience, cognitive psychology, artificial intelligence, and philosophy of mind. I interviewed researchers, educators, and practitioners who are grappling with the implications of AI for human cognition. I examined case studies of AI failures and successes, looking for patterns that might reveal the true nature of machine intelligence and its effects on human thinking.

What emerged from this investigation was a picture of profound transformation. We are not simply adopting new tools; we are undergoing a fundamental reorganization of human cognitive architecture. The boundaries between human and artificial intelligence are becoming increasingly blurred, creating new forms of hybrid cognition that combine human wisdom with machine processing power. This transformation offers unprecedented opportunities for enhancing human capability while simultaneously creating new risks and challenges that we are only beginning to understand.

The concept of "prompted minds" emerged from this research as a way to describe the contemporary human condition. We are increasingly living in a state of consciousness that is shaped by interactions with artificial intelligence systems. Every time we search for information, ask a question to an AI assistant, or rely on algorithmic recommendations, we are participating in a form of cognitive collaboration that influences not only what we know but how we think.

This collaboration is so pervasive and seamless that it often occurs below the threshold of conscious awareness. We have become prompted minds—human consciousnesses that are continuously shaped by AI interactions—without fully recognizing the implications of this transformation. The challenge is learning to navigate this new cognitive landscape with wisdom and intentionality.

The title of this book reflects three interconnected themes that run throughout our exploration. "Cognition" refers to the fundamental processes of thinking, learning, and knowing that define human consciousness. "Offloading" describes the process by which we transfer cognitive tasks to external systems, from ancient writing systems to modern AI assistants. "The Illusion of AI Understanding" captures the central paradox of our time: AI systems that can simulate understanding so convincingly that we often mistake computational processing for genuine comprehension.

Together, these themes reveal how context, bias, and models are shaping the future of thinking itself. The AI systems we interact with are not neutral tools but embody particular contexts, biases, and models of understanding that influence our own cognitive processes. Understanding these influences is crucial for maintaining agency and wisdom in an increasingly AI-augmented world.

This book is written for anyone who wants to understand the cognitive transformation we are experiencing and learn to navigate it thoughtfully. Whether you are an educator wondering how to prepare students for an AI-augmented future, a professional seeking to collaborate effectively with AI systems, or simply a curious individual trying to understand how AI is changing human consciousness, this book offers insights and frameworks for approaching these challenges.

The journey we will take together spans nine chapters that build upon each other to create a comprehensive understanding of the prompted mind. We will explore the historical evolution of cognitive tools, examine the architecture of artificial intelligence, investigate the illusions of understanding that AI systems create, and analyze the biases and limitations that shape AI behavior. We will look at how AI is transforming human cognition itself, consider the future possibilities for cognitive enhancement and hybrid intelligence, and develop practical strategies for navigating AI-augmented environments.

Throughout this exploration, we will maintain a balanced perspective that neither celebrates AI uncritically nor dismisses its potential. The goal is not to resist the cognitive transformation we are experiencing but to understand it deeply enough to guide it in directions that enhance rather than diminish human flourishing. This requires honest acknowledgment of both the opportunities and risks created by AI, along with practical wisdom for navigating the challenges ahead.

The question that started this journey—whether AI systems truly understand what they tell us—remains central to our exploration. But it has evolved into a broader inquiry about the nature of understanding itself and how human and artificial intelligence can work together to create new forms of cognitive capability. The answer, as we will discover, is not simple. But the journey toward understanding is essential for anyone who wants to thrive in an age of prompted minds.

As we embark on this exploration together, I invite you to approach it with both curiosity and critical thinking. The transformation we are examining is not happening to us but with us. We are active participants in shaping the future of human cognition, and the choices we make about how to interact with AI systems will determine whether this transformation enhances or diminishes our humanity.

The future of thinking is not predetermined. It emerges from the decisions we make about how to design, deploy, and interact with artificial intelligence. By understanding the implications of the prompted mind, we can work toward a future where AI amplifies the best of human intelligence while preserving the qualities that make us uniquely human.

The journey begins now.

Yours, Roger

Chapter 1: The Cognitive Handoff

In the ancient Greek play Prometheus Bound, Aeschylus tells the story of the Titan who stole fire from the gods and gave it to humanity. Among Prometheus's gifts to our species was not just fire itself, but the ability to write—to externalize thought and memory onto clay tablets and papyrus scrolls [1]. This mythological account captures a profound truth about human nature: we have always been creatures who extend our minds beyond the boundaries of our skulls, using tools and technologies to amplify our cognitive capabilities.

Today, as we stand at the threshold of an artificial intelligence revolution, we find ourselves once again receiving a Promethean gift. Large language models like ChatGPT, Claude, and GPT-4 represent the latest and most sophisticated cognitive prosthetics in human history. Yet unlike the clay tablets of ancient Mesopotamia or the calculators of the 20th century, these AI systems don't merely store information or perform calculations—they appear to think, reason, and understand. This appearance of intelligence creates both unprecedented opportunities and profound risks for human cognition.

The central thesis of this book is that we are witnessing a fundamental transformation in the relationship between human minds and external cognitive tools. As we increasingly delegate thinking tasks to AI systems, we risk creating what researchers have termed "illusions of understanding"—the false belief that we comprehend more about the world than we actually do [2]. These illusions emerge from the very sophistication of AI systems that makes them so appealing: their ability to generate coherent, contextually appropriate responses that mask the absence of genuine understanding.

This cognitive handoff—the transfer of thinking tasks from human minds to artificial systems—represents both the culmination of a process that began with the first writing systems and a qualitative leap into uncharted territory. Unlike previous cognitive tools that extended specific mental capabilities, AI systems promise to augment or replace general intelligence itself. Understanding this transition requires examining both the psychological mechanisms that drive cognitive offloading and the unique characteristics of AI systems that make them particularly seductive and potentially dangerous cognitive partners.

The Historical Evolution of Cognitive Tools

To understand the significance of our current moment, we must first trace the long history of human cognitive enhancement through external tools. The development of writing systems around 3400 BCE in the Sumer region of Mesopotamia marked the first major revolution in human cognitive capabilities [1]. The Sumerian script, known as Cuneiform, emerged from the practical constraints of available materials—clay tablets and reed styluses—demonstrating how the physical properties of our tools shape the structure of our thoughts.

As archaeologist Lambros Malafouris has argued, these early writing systems did more than simply record information; they fundamentally restructured how humans processed and organized knowledge [1]. The Linear B tablets used by the Mycenaeans around 1400 BCE provide a compelling example of this cognitive restructuring. These clay tablets came in two distinct forms: small leaf-shaped tablets for initial records and larger page-shaped tablets for consolidated information. Because corrections could not be made once the clay dried, scribes developed elaborate filing systems, creating multiple small tablets that would later be synthesized onto larger ones.

This process, Malafouris observes, externalized and restructured information processing in ways that would have been impossible within the confines of human memory alone. The spatial and temporal constraints of the medium forced users to develop new cognitive strategies for organizing and retrieving information. As he notes, "The Mycenaean simply reads what the Linear B tablet remembers. In fact, being able to read, that person no longer needs to remember" [1].

This insight reveals a fundamental principle of cognitive offloading: external tools don't merely supplement human memory and reasoning—they transform them. The introduction of alphabetic writing systems in the 8th century BCE, adopted from the Phoenicians, further accelerated this transformation by making literacy more accessible and flexible. Each technological advancement in writing—from clay tablets to papyrus, from scrolls to codices, from handwriting to printing—created new possibilities for human thought while simultaneously making certain cognitive skills less necessary.

The pattern established by writing systems has repeated throughout human history. The invention of the printing press in the 15th century democratized access to information while reducing the cultural importance of memorization. The development of mechanical calculators in the 17th century began the process of offloading mathematical computation. The introduction of personal computers in the late 20th century accelerated cognitive offloading across multiple domains, from word processing to data analysis.

Each of these technological transitions followed a similar trajectory. Initial resistance gave way to gradual adoption, followed by widespread integration and, ultimately, cognitive dependence. Socrates famously worried that writing would weaken human memory, arguing in Plato's Phaedrus that external records would make people "forgetful" because they would "rely on writing to bring things to their remembrance from outside themselves" rather than developing internal recall. His concerns, while prescient in some ways, failed to anticipate the cognitive benefits that would emerge from freeing human memory for higher-order thinking tasks.

The key insight from this historical perspective is that cognitive offloading is not a recent phenomenon but a defining characteristic of human intelligence. What makes our current moment unique is not the fact of cognitive offloading itself, but rather the sophistication and apparent autonomy of the systems to which we are delegating cognitive tasks. Previous tools required human operators to understand their limitations and actively direct their use. AI systems, by contrast, can operate with minimal human oversight and often produce outputs that exceed human capabilities in specific domains.

The Psychological Foundations of Cognitive Offloading

Understanding why humans so readily delegate cognitive tasks to external systems requires examining the psychological mechanisms that drive this behavior. Cognitive offloading, defined as "our reliance on the external environment in order to reduce cognitive demand," is not simply a matter of convenience—it reflects fundamental aspects of how human minds operate and adapt to their environments [3].

Research by Xiao Hu, Liang Luo, and Stephen Fleming has revealed that cognitive offloading decisions are closely tied to metacognitive processes—our awareness and understanding of our own cognitive capabilities [3]. In their experiments, participants were asked to learn word pairs and decide whether to "save" some pairs on a computer for later retrieval. The results demonstrated that people adaptively saved the most difficult items and used this offloaded information to boost their memory performance. Crucially, participants' confidence judgments about their memory predicted their decisions to use the saved information, indicating that cognitive offloading is intimately connected to metacognitive evaluation.

This finding illuminates a critical aspect of human psychology: we offload cognitive tasks not randomly, but strategically, based on our assessment of our own capabilities and the reliability of external systems. The researchers developed a Bayesian computational model showing that beliefs about the performance boost gained from using offloaded information are negatively coupled to an evaluation of memory ability. In other words, the less confident we are in our own cognitive abilities, the more likely we are to rely on external systems.

This metacognitive dimension of cognitive offloading helps explain why AI systems are particularly seductive cognitive partners. Unlike traditional tools that require explicit activation and direction, AI systems can anticipate our needs and provide assistance before we even recognize that we need it. When ChatGPT completes our sentences or suggests improvements to our writing, it creates a feedback loop that can gradually erode our confidence in our own capabilities while simultaneously increasing our reliance on the system.

The concept of active externalism, developed by philosophers Andy Clark and David Chalmers, provides a theoretical framework for understanding how external tools become integrated into our cognitive processes [4]. In their influential paper "The Extended Mind," Clark and Chalmers argue that cognitive processes can extend beyond the boundaries of the brain to include external tools and technologies. They illustrate this concept through a thought experiment involving three scenarios: a person mentally rotating geometric shapes, the same person using a computer interface to physically rotate the shapes, and a person in a hypothetical future using a neural implant to perform the rotation.

Clark and Chalmers argue that all three scenarios involve fundamentally similar cognitive processes, despite the fact that the second involves external manipulation and the third involves technological augmentation. The key insight is that the location of cognitive processing—whether internal or external—is less important than the functional role it plays in achieving cognitive goals. As they put it, "Cognitive processes ain't (all) in the head!" [4].

This perspective has profound implications for understanding human-AI interaction. When we use AI systems to help us write, analyze data, or solve problems, we are not simply using tools—we are creating extended cognitive systems in which human and artificial intelligence become functionally integrated. The boundaries between self and system become blurred, making it increasingly difficult to distinguish between our own capabilities and those of our AI partners.

The psychological appeal of this integration is evident in recent research on AI as cognitive prosthetics. Daniel Graham argues that AI systems like ChatGPT function most effectively not as enhancers of already high intelligence, but as equalizers that help those with lower cognitive abilities reach average performance levels [5]. This "cognitive prosthetic" model suggests that AI systems approximate normal cognitive function in much the same way that physical prosthetics approximate normal physical function.

The prosthetic metaphor is particularly apt because it captures both the benefits and limitations of AI assistance. Just as a prosthetic limb enables mobility while requiring removal in certain contexts (such as showering), AI systems provide cognitive assistance while remaining unsuitable for all situations. The challenge lies in developing the metacognitive awareness necessary to recognize when AI assistance is appropriate and when it might be counterproductive or even harmful.

From Simple Tools to Intelligent Agents

The transition from traditional cognitive tools to AI systems represents a qualitative shift in the nature of human-technology interaction. Previous cognitive tools, from abacuses to calculators to word processors, were fundamentally passive instruments that required human direction and interpretation. Users understood the limitations of these tools and maintained clear boundaries between their own capabilities and those of their instruments. A calculator could perform arithmetic operations with perfect accuracy, but it could not understand the meaning of the calculations or suggest alternative approaches to a problem.

AI systems, particularly large language models, blur these boundaries in unprecedented ways. They can engage in seemingly intelligent conversation, provide explanations for their reasoning, and even express uncertainty about their own capabilities. This apparent intelligence creates what researchers Lisa Messeri and M.J. Crockett have termed "illusions of understanding"—the false belief that we understand more about the world than we actually do [2].

These illusions emerge from the sophisticated ways in which AI systems can exploit human cognitive limitations. When an AI system provides a detailed explanation of a complex phenomenon, complete with technical terminology and logical structure, it can create a powerful sense of comprehension in the user, even when the explanation is incomplete, biased, or fundamentally flawed. The coherence and confidence of AI-generated content can override our natural skepticism and critical thinking processes.

Messeri and Crockett argue that this dynamic poses particular risks for scientific research and knowledge production. As they observe, "The proliferation of AI tools in science risks introducing a phase of scientific enquiry in which we produce more but understand less" [2]. This concern extends beyond academic research to encompass all domains where AI systems are used to augment human reasoning and decision-making.

The seductive power of AI systems lies partly in their ability to provide what appears to be objective, comprehensive analysis while actually reflecting the biases and limitations of their training data and algorithms. Unlike human experts, who typically signal their uncertainty and acknowledge the limitations of their knowledge, AI systems often present information with a confidence that can be misleading. This confidence can lead users to accept AI-generated content without the critical evaluation they would apply to human-produced information.

The problem is compounded by the fact that AI systems can generate content that is simultaneously impressive and subtly flawed. A language model might produce an eloquent essay on climate change that demonstrates sophisticated understanding of the scientific literature while containing factual errors or logical inconsistencies that are difficult for non-experts to detect. The overall quality of the output can mask these specific deficiencies, leading readers to overestimate both the accuracy of the information and their own understanding of the topic.

This dynamic creates what we might call "cognitive inflation"—an artificial enhancement of our sense of knowledge and capability that is not matched by actual understanding. Unlike the cognitive offloading that occurs with traditional tools, where users typically maintain awareness of their dependence on external systems, AI-mediated cognitive inflation can occur without conscious recognition. Users may genuinely believe they have learned something new or developed deeper insights when they have actually become more dependent on AI assistance without gaining substantive knowledge.

The implications of this shift extend beyond individual cognition to encompass broader social and cultural dynamics. When large numbers of people rely on AI systems for information and analysis, there is a risk of creating what Messeri and Crockett call "scientific monocultures"—environments where certain types of methods, questions, and viewpoints come to dominate alternative approaches [2]. This homogenization can make entire fields of knowledge less innovative and more vulnerable to systematic errors.

The challenge facing contemporary society is learning to harness the genuine benefits of AI systems while avoiding the cognitive traps they can create. This requires developing new forms of digital literacy that go beyond traditional computer skills to encompass understanding of how AI systems work, what their limitations are, and how they can influence human thinking in subtle but significant ways.

Contemporary Examples and Implications

The cognitive handoff to AI systems is already well underway across multiple domains of human activity. In education, students increasingly rely on AI writing assistants to help compose essays and research papers, often without fully understanding the content they are submitting. In healthcare, diagnostic AI systems can identify patterns in medical imaging that exceed human capabilities, but their recommendations may be based on correlations that lack clear causal explanations. In business, AI-powered analytics tools can process vast amounts of data to identify trends and opportunities, but their insights may reflect biases present in historical data rather than genuine predictive value.

Each of these applications demonstrates both the promise and the peril of cognitive offloading to AI systems. The promise lies in the genuine enhancement of human capabilities—AI can help students organize their thoughts more clearly, assist doctors in identifying subtle diagnostic signs, and enable business analysts to process information at unprecedented scale. The peril lies in the potential for these systems to create illusions of understanding that mask fundamental gaps in knowledge and reasoning.

Consider the example of AI-assisted writing, which has become increasingly common in academic and professional contexts. When a student uses an AI system to help structure an argument or improve the clarity of their prose, they may genuinely benefit from the assistance. However, if the AI system generates content that the student does not fully understand or cannot independently reproduce, the apparent improvement in their writing may mask a lack of genuine learning. The student may receive positive feedback on their AI-assisted work while failing to develop the critical thinking and communication skills that the assignment was designed to foster.

This dynamic is particularly concerning in educational contexts because it can create a feedback loop that undermines the development of independent thinking capabilities. Students who become accustomed to AI assistance may find it increasingly difficult to work without such support, leading to a form of cognitive dependence that persists beyond their formal education. The long-term implications of this trend are still unclear, but they raise important questions about how educational institutions should adapt their practices to account for the availability of AI assistance.

Similar concerns arise in professional contexts where AI systems are used to augment human decision-making. Recent research by Megan Kelly and Evan Risko has shown that when people know they can rely on external memory stores like internet access, they are less likely to devote time to studying information and using strategies like mnemonics to memorize what they have learned [1]. This finding suggests that the availability of AI assistance may reduce motivation for developing and maintaining cognitive skills, even when such skills would be valuable for independent reasoning and problem-solving.

The challenge is compounded by the fact that AI systems often excel in precisely those areas where human cognitive limitations are most apparent. Large language models can process and synthesize information from thousands of sources simultaneously, identify subtle patterns in complex datasets, and generate coherent explanations for phenomena that would require extensive research for humans to understand. These capabilities can create a sense that AI systems are not merely tools but genuine intellectual partners capable of independent thought and insight.

This anthropomorphization of AI systems—the tendency to attribute human-like qualities such as understanding, intention, and consciousness to artificial systems—represents another dimension of the cognitive handoff phenomenon. When we begin to think of AI systems as intelligent agents rather than sophisticated tools, we may be more likely to defer to their judgments and less likely to maintain the critical distance necessary for effective human-AI collaboration.

The implications of these trends extend beyond individual cognition to encompass broader questions about the future of human knowledge and expertise. If AI systems become sufficiently capable of performing tasks that currently require human intelligence, what happens to the cognitive skills and knowledge that have traditionally defined human expertise? Will future generations develop the same capacity for independent reasoning and critical thinking that has characterized human intelligence throughout history, or will they become increasingly dependent on AI assistance for complex cognitive tasks?

These questions do not have simple answers, but they highlight the importance of approaching the cognitive handoff to AI systems with both enthusiasm and caution. The goal should not be to reject AI assistance entirely—the benefits are too significant and the technology too powerful to ignore. Instead, the challenge is to develop frameworks for human-AI collaboration that preserve human agency and cognitive autonomy while leveraging the genuine advantages that AI systems can provide.

In Conclusion

The cognitive handoff to AI systems represents both the culmination of a long historical process and the beginning of a new chapter in human cognitive evolution. From the clay tablets of ancient Mesopotamia to the large language models of today, humans have consistently sought to extend their mental capabilities through external tools and technologies. Each major technological transition has brought both opportunities and challenges, requiring societies to adapt their practices and institutions to account for new cognitive possibilities.

What makes our current moment unique is not the fact of cognitive offloading itself, but rather the sophistication and apparent autonomy of the systems to which we are delegating cognitivc tasks. AI systems can engage in seemingly intelligent conversation, provide detailed explanations for complex phenomena, and generate content that often exceeds human capabilities in specific domains. This apparent intelligence creates powerful illusions of understanding that can mask fundamental gaps in knowledge and reasoning.

The challenge facing contemporary society is learning to navigate this new cognitive landscape in ways that preserve human agency and intellectual autonomy while leveraging the genuine benefits that AI systems can provide. This requires developing new forms of digital literacy that encompass not only technical skills but also metacognitive awareness—the ability to recognize when AI assistance is appropriate and when it might be counterproductive.

The stakes of this challenge are high. If we succeed in developing effective frameworks for human-AI collaboration, we may be able to augment human intelligence in ways that enhance creativity, accelerate scientific discovery, and improve decision-making across multiple domains. If we fail to maintain appropriate boundaries and critical distance, we risk creating a future in which human cognitive capabilities atrophy while our dependence on AI systems grows ever stronger.

The following chapters will explore these themes in greater detail, examining the specific mechanisms through which AI systems create illusions of understanding, the biases and limitations that shape their outputs, and the strategies that individuals and institutions can employ to maintain cognitive autonomy in an AI-augmented world. The goal is not to provide definitive answers to questions that are still evolving, but rather to develop frameworks for thinking about these issues that can guide us as we navigate the cognitive transformations ahead.

As we stand at this technological crossroads, we would do well to remember the lesson of Prometheus: the gifts of technology are double-edged, bringing both enlightenment and risk. Our task is to approach these gifts with the wisdom necessary to harness their benefits while avoiding their potential dangers. The future of human thinking depends on our ability to maintain this delicate balance.

CHAPTER 1

THE COGNITIVE HANDOFF

The history, psychology and impact of how we offload thinking to tools—and what it means for the future.

CHAPTER AT A GLANCE

HISTORICAL EVOLUTION OF COGNITIVE TOOLS
From memory aids and writing to digital devices and AI—tools have always extended our thinking.

PSYCHOLOGICAL FOUNDATIONS
Cognitive offloading reduces mental load, optimizes resources, and shapes how we think and remember.

CONTEMPORARY EXAMPLES
Smartphones, search engines, and AI assistants are now central to how we learn, decide and create.

IMPLICATIONS
Offloading brings power and convenience—but also dependency and vulnerability of our cognition.

KEY TAKEAWAYS

1. **TOOLS SHAPE MINDS**
Every cognitive tool we adopt reshapes how we think, remember and solve problems.

2. **OFFLOADING REDUCES COGNITIVE LOAD**
By shifting effort to external tools, we free mental resources for other tasks—but at a cost.

3. **BENEFITS COME WITH TRADE-OFFS**
Efficiency and access increase, while deep understanding, retention and independence may decline.

4. **AWARENESS IS OUR ADVANTAGE**
Understanding the dynamics of offloading allows us to design better tools—and remain the pilot of our minds.

THE EVOLUTION OF COGNITIVE TOOLS

- **PREHISTORIC MEMORY AIDS** Externalizing memory in marks and symbols.
- **WRITING & RECORD KEEPING** Capturing knowledge across time and space.
- **PRINTING PRESS** Scaling knowledge and standardizing information.
- **DIGITAL REVOLUTION** Storing, accessing and searching information instantly.
- **AI & BEYOND** Delegating complex cognition to intelligent systems.

VISUAL FOCUS

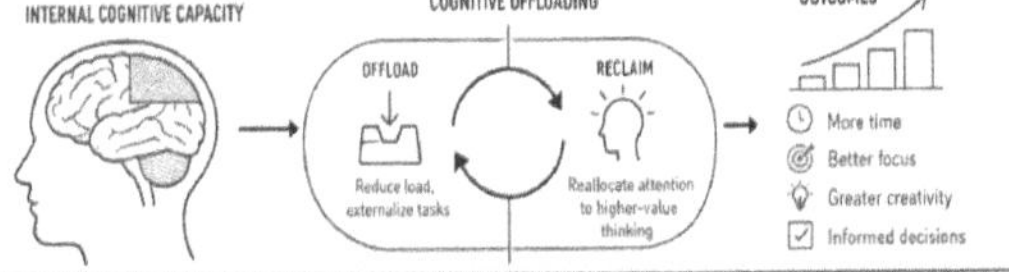

> *We do not just use tools. We become different thinkers because of them. The future belongs to those who understand this handoff.*

REFERENCES

[1] Jensen, K. (2023, November 5). How the development of writing systems changed the way our brains work, and how modern technology is changing it again. *Retrospect Journal*. https://retrospectjournal.com/2023/11/05/how-the-development-of-writing-systems-changed-the-way-our-brains-work-and-how-modern-technology-is-changing-it-again/

[2] Messeri, L., & Crockett, M. J. (2024). Artificial intelligence and illusions of understanding in scientific research. *Nature*, 627, 49-58. https://doi.org/10.1038/s41586-024-07146-0

[3] Hu, X., Luo, L., & Fleming, S. M. (2019). A role for metamemory in cognitive offloading. *Cognition*, 193, 104012. https://doi.org/10.1016/j.cognition.2019.104012

[4] Clark, A., & Chalmers, D. (1998). The extended mind. *Analysis*, 58(1), 7-19.

[5] Graham, D. (2023, June 7). Could ChatGPT be a cognitive prosthesis? *Psychology Today*. https://www.psychologytoday.com/us/blog/your-internet-brain/202306/could-chatgpt-be-a-cognitive-prosthesis

Chapter 2: The Architecture of Artificial Understanding

When we interact with a large language model like ChatGPT or Claude, we encounter something unprecedented in the history of human-machine interaction: a system that appears to understand our questions, engage in sophisticated reasoning, and provide thoughtful responses that often exceed our expectations. The fluency and apparent intelligence of these systems can be so compelling that we naturally attribute to them the same kind of understanding we experience in human conversation. Yet beneath this veneer of comprehension lies a fundamentally different kind of information processing—one that challenges our most basic assumptions about the nature of understanding itself.

This chapter examines the architecture of artificial intelligence systems, particularly large language models, to understand how they create such convincing illusions of understanding while operating through mechanisms that are fundamentally different from human cognition. By exploring the technical foundations of these systems—from transformer architectures to attention mechanisms—we can begin to appreciate both their remarkable capabilities and their profound limitations. More importantly, we can develop a clearer picture of what it means for a system to "understand" something, and why the distinction between statistical pattern matching and genuine comprehension matters for how we interact with AI systems.

The central argument of this chapter is that current AI systems, despite their impressive performance, operate through sophisticated statistical pattern matching rather than genuine understanding. They excel at identifying correlations in vast datasets and generating contextually appropriate responses, but they lack the semantic grounding and causal reasoning that characterize human understanding. This distinction is not merely academic—it has profound implications for how we should interpret AI outputs, what tasks we should delegate to these systems, and how we can avoid the cognitive traps that their apparent intelligence creates.

Understanding the architecture of artificial intelligence requires examining both the technical mechanisms that enable these systems to function and the philosophical questions they raise about the nature of understanding itself. As we will see, the gap between computational processing and genuine comprehension is not simply a matter of scale or sophistication—it reflects fundamental differences in how artificial and human intelligence operate.

The Transformer Revolution: Attention as the Foundation of Artificial Intelligence

The modern era of artificial intelligence can be traced to a single paper published in 2017 with the provocative title "Attention Is All You Need." This work introduced the transformer architecture, which has since become the foundation for virtually all state-of-the-art language models, from GPT-4 to Claude to Gemini. To understand how these systems create such convincing illusions of understanding, we must first examine the technical mechanisms that make them possible.

At its core, an attention mechanism is "a machine learning technique that directs deep learning models to prioritize (or attend to) the most relevant parts of input data" [1]. This seemingly simple concept represents a fundamental breakthrough in how artificial systems process information.

Unlike previous approaches that processed data sequentially or through fixed patterns, attention mechanisms allow AI systems to examine entire sequences simultaneously and dynamically determine which parts deserve the most focus.

The inspiration for attention mechanisms comes from human cognition itself. As humans, we constantly engage in selective attention, focusing on salient details while filtering out irrelevant information. When reading a complex sentence, we don't give equal weight to every word—we naturally emphasize key terms, relationships, and concepts that are most relevant to understanding the overall meaning. Attention mechanisms attempt to replicate this cognitive process computationally.

Mathematically, attention mechanisms compute "attention weights" that reflect the relative importance of each part of an input sequence to the task at hand [1]. These weights are then applied to increase or decrease the influence of each part of the input according to its calculated importance. The system learns to assign accurate attention weights through training on large datasets, gradually developing the ability to identify which elements of a sequence are most relevant for generating appropriate responses.

The revolutionary nature of the transformer architecture becomes clear when we compare it to earlier approaches. Before transformers, the dominant paradigm for processing sequential data relied on recurrent neural networks (RNNs), which processed information step by step in a serialized manner. This approach created significant limitations: RNNs struggled to identify dependencies between elements that were far apart in a sequence, and their sequential nature made them difficult to parallelize efficiently.

Consider the challenge of machine translation, which was one of the first applications where attention mechanisms proved transformative. Earlier systems used an encoder-decoder architecture where the encoder would process an entire source sentence and compress it into a single "context vector" that captured the meaning of the whole sentence. The decoder would then use this fixed-length vector to generate the translation word by word. This approach created an information bottleneck—complex sentences had to be compressed into the same amount of space as simple ones, and information from early parts of the sentence would often be lost by the time the decoder reached the end.

Attention mechanisms solved this problem by allowing the decoder to access every hidden state from the encoder, not just the final compressed representation. At each step of translation, the attention mechanism would determine which words in the source sentence were most relevant for generating the next word in the target language. This eliminated the information bottleneck and dramatically improved translation quality, especially for longer sentences.

The transformer architecture took this concept even further by building entire models around attention mechanisms. Instead of using recurrent connections or convolutions, transformers rely exclusively on attention layers combined with standard feedforward networks. This design provides several crucial advantages: flexibility over both time and space (the ability to identify dependencies regardless of distance), and massive parallelization that takes full advantage of modern GPU architectures [1].

The result is a system that can process vast amounts of text simultaneously, identifying complex patterns and relationships that would be impossible for earlier architectures to detect. When we interact with a large language model, we are witnessing the output of billions of attention calculations, each one determining which parts of the input are most relevant for generating the next piece of the response.

Statistical Pattern Matching vs. Semantic Understanding

While the technical sophistication of transformer architectures is undeniable, understanding their capabilities requires examining what these systems actually do when they process information. Despite their impressive performance, large language models operate through what is fundamentally statistical pattern matching rather than genuine semantic understanding. This distinction, while subtle, has profound implications for how we interpret their outputs and integrate them into human cognitive processes.

The difference between statistical and semantic processing becomes clear when we consider how humans and machines approach the same task. When humans learn language, they connect patterns to "high order semantic abstractions of the underlying objects and activities" [2]. Our background knowledge and life experiences provide the necessary context to reason about patterns and identify those most likely to represent robust, actionable knowledge. We understand not just what words typically follow other words, but why those relationships exist and what they mean in the broader context of our experience.

Machines, by contrast, "blindly search for the strongest signals in a pile of data" [2]. Lacking the cushion of background knowledge or life experiences that humans possess, deep learning algorithms cannot distinguish between meaningful and spurious indicators. They "merely blindly encode the world according to statistics, rather than semantics," relying on primitive patterns rather than semantic abstractions [2].

This fundamental difference can be illustrated through a thought experiment. Imagine showing a human and an AI system the sentence "The bank was steep and muddy." A human immediately understands that "bank" refers to the side of a river, not a financial institution, because they possess semantic knowledge about rivers, mud, and the physical world. They can visualize the scene and understand the causal relationships that make a riverbank steep and muddy.

An AI system, however, arrives at the correct interpretation through an entirely different process. It has learned from millions of examples that when "bank" appears near words like "steep" and "muddy," it typically refers to a riverbank rather than a financial institution. The system can generate the correct response without any understanding of what rivers are, why their banks might be steep, or what mud actually is. It operates through statistical correlation rather than semantic comprehension.

Kalev Leetaru captures this distinction perfectly when he describes AI systems as "akin to a human shown patterns in a pile of numbers and asked to flag future occurrences without any understanding of what those numbers represent or what the decision involves" [2]. This analogy illuminates why current AI systems can be simultaneously impressive and brittle—they excel at identifying patterns that humans might miss, but they lack the semantic grounding necessary to understand when those patterns are meaningful versus spurious.

The brittleness of statistical pattern matching becomes apparent in the "great contradiction of deep learning": systems that "perform at superhuman levels much of the time, only to spectacularly fail at any moment in the most unexpected and counterintuitive ways" [2]. These failures occur because the systems "search for correlations in data, rather than meaning." When they encounter situations that fall outside their training distribution or involve novel combinations of familiar elements, they can produce outputs that are statistically plausible but semantically nonsensical.

This limitation has serious implications for high-stakes applications. As Leetaru notes, the statistical nature of AI decision-making makes "life-and-death applications of machine learning like driverless cars so frightening, in that we have no idea what basic scenario might cause them to suddenly fail, potentially with fatal consequences" [2]. The same principle applies to any domain where AI systems are used to augment human reasoning—we cannot predict when their statistical approach will lead them astray because we cannot fully understand the correlations they have learned to rely upon.

The challenge is compounded by the fact that AI systems often excel precisely in those areas where statistical approaches can identify subtle patterns that escape human notice. In domains where observational data has historically been sparse, machine learning can discover legitimate signals that human theories have missed. This creates a paradox: the very capabilities that make AI systems valuable also make them difficult to validate and potentially dangerous to rely upon without appropriate safeguards.

Understanding this distinction between statistical and semantic processing is crucial for developing appropriate frameworks for human-AI collaboration. It suggests that the goal should not be to replace human understanding with artificial intelligence, but rather to develop systems that can "reason about the world in terms of semantics, rather than statistics and incorporate external world knowledge and context into their decision-making processes" [2]. Until such systems are developed, we must remain cognizant of the fundamental limitations of statistical pattern matching, no matter how sophisticated it becomes.

The Chinese Room and the Symbol Grounding Problem

The philosophical foundations for understanding the limitations of artificial intelligence were established decades before the first transformer was conceived. In 1980, philosopher John Searle introduced what has become known as the Chinese Room argument, a thought experiment that directly challenges the notion that computational processes can produce genuine understanding [3]. This argument remains remarkably relevant to contemporary discussions about large language models and their apparent intelligence.

Searle's thought experiment asks us to imagine an English speaker sitting in a room with a comprehensive set of rules for manipulating Chinese characters. The person receives Chinese characters through a slot, follows the English instructions to manipulate these symbols, and sends back appropriate Chinese responses. From the outside, it appears that the person in the room understands Chinese—they can engage in sophisticated conversations and provide contextually appropriate responses. However, the person following the rules has no understanding of Chinese whatsoever; they are simply manipulating symbols according to syntactic rules without any comprehension of their semantic meaning [3].

The parallel to modern AI systems is striking. Large language models operate by following computational rules for manipulating tokens (linguistic symbols) based on patterns learned from training data. Like the person in the Chinese

Room, these systems can produce remarkably sophisticated outputs that appear to demonstrate understanding, but they are fundamentally engaged in symbol manipulation without semantic comprehension. They process syntax—the formal structure of language—without access to semantics—the meaning that language conveys.

Searle's argument was specifically directed at what he termed "Strong AI"—the view that "suitably programmed computers (or the programs themselves) can understand natural language and actually have other mental capabilities similar to the humans whose behavior they mimic" [3]. This position holds that computers don't merely simulate intelligence; they actually possess it. The Chinese Room argument challenges this view by demonstrating that symbol manipulation, no matter how sophisticated, cannot constitute genuine understanding.

The formal structure of Searle's argument can be expressed as a reductio ad absurdum: If Strong AI is true, then there exists a program such that any system running that program would thereby understand language. However, a human could run such a program (as in the Chinese Room scenario) without gaining understanding of the language. Therefore, Strong AI must be false [3]. The conclusion is that "running a program cannot endow the system with language understanding."

This philosophical insight connects to a broader problem in cognitive science known as the symbol grounding problem. This challenge concerns how symbols or representations in a computational system can acquire meaning beyond their formal relationships to other symbols. In human cognition, our symbols are grounded in sensorimotor experience, emotional associations, and embodied interaction with the world. When we use the word "red," it connects to visual experiences, emotional associations, and countless contextual memories that give the symbol rich semantic content.

AI systems, by contrast, work with symbols that are grounded only in statistical relationships to other symbols. A language model's representation of "red" is based entirely on how that token relates to other tokens in its training data—it has no visual experience of redness, no emotional associations with red objects, and no embodied understanding of what redness means in the physical world. The symbol exists in a closed system of linguistic relationships without external grounding.

This limitation becomes apparent when we consider how AI systems handle novel situations or concepts that require genuine understanding rather than pattern matching. While a human can reason about hypothetical scenarios, understand metaphors, or apply knowledge creatively to new domains, AI systems are fundamentally constrained by the statistical patterns present in their training data. They cannot truly understand what they are processing because their symbols lack the semantic grounding that makes understanding possible.

The implications of the Chinese Room argument for contemporary AI are profound. As Searle noted, the argument suggests that "computers merely use syntactic rules to manipulate symbol strings, but have no understanding of meaning or semantics" [3]. This insight remains valid regardless of how sophisticated the syntactic manipulation becomes. Even if future AI systems become vastly more capable at pattern matching and symbol manipulation, they will not thereby achieve genuine understanding unless they solve the fundamental problem of symbol grounding.

The relevance of these philosophical insights extends beyond academic debate. If AI systems operate through sophisticated symbol manipulation rather than genuine understanding, then their outputs must be interpreted differently than we would interpret the statements of a human expert. Their apparent confidence and fluency can mask fundamental gaps in comprehension that may not become apparent until the system encounters situations that require genuine semantic understanding rather than statistical pattern matching.

This does not diminish the remarkable capabilities of current AI systems, but it does suggest that we should approach them with appropriate epistemic humility. They are powerful tools for pattern recognition and symbol manipulation, but they are not thinking beings in the way that humans are. Understanding this distinction is crucial for developing appropriate frameworks for human-AI collaboration and avoiding the cognitive traps that their apparent intelligence can create.

Emergent Behaviors and the Scaling Hypothesis

One of the most intriguing aspects of large language models is their apparent development of capabilities that were not explicitly programmed or anticipated by their creators. As these systems have grown larger and been trained on more data, they have begun to exhibit what researchers call "emergent behaviors"—abilities that seem to arise spontaneously from the complex interactions of their underlying components. These emergent capabilities include few-shot learning, chain-of-thought reasoning, and the ability to perform tasks that were never explicitly included in their training objectives.

The phenomenon of emergence in AI systems presents a fascinating puzzle for our understanding of artificial intelligence. When GPT-3 demonstrated the ability to write poetry, solve mathematical problems, and engage in creative reasoning with minimal examples, it appeared to have developed genuine cognitive capabilities that transcended simple pattern matching. These behaviors seemed to suggest that sufficiently large and sophisticated AI systems might indeed achieve something approaching genuine understanding.

However, the appearance of emergent behaviors does not necessarily indicate the presence of genuine understanding. Instead, these capabilities may represent increasingly sophisticated forms of statistical pattern matching that become possible when systems reach sufficient scale and complexity. The transformer architecture's ability to identify subtle patterns across vast datasets means that larger models can detect correlations and relationships that smaller systems miss entirely.

Consider the phenomenon of few-shot learning, where a language model can learn to perform a new task from just a few examples. This capability appears to demonstrate genuine learning and adaptation, suggesting that the system understands the underlying principles of the task. However, a more parsimonious explanation is that the model has learned to recognize patterns that indicate what type of task is being requested and can then apply statistical patterns from its training data to generate appropriate responses.

The scaling hypothesis—the idea that many AI capabilities improve predictably with increases in model size, data, and computational resources—provides important insights into the nature of these emergent behaviors. If AI capabilities were based on genuine understanding, we might expect to see qualitative leaps or discontinuous improvements as systems cross certain thresholds of comprehension. Instead, most capabilities appear to improve smoothly and predictably with scale, suggesting that they emerge from quantitative improvements in pattern matching rather than qualitative changes in understanding.

This perspective is supported by the observation that AI systems often fail in ways that would be impossible if they possessed genuine understanding of their domains. A language model might demonstrate sophisticated reasoning about physics in one context while making elementary errors in another, or it might generate mathematically elegant solutions to complex problems while failing to recognize obvious contradictions in its own outputs. These inconsistencies suggest that the system's apparent capabilities are based on statistical patterns rather than coherent understanding.

The implications of emergent behaviors for human-AI interaction are complex. On one hand, these capabilities make AI systems increasingly useful for a wide range of tasks, from creative writing to scientific research. The ability of large language models to engage in sophisticated reasoning and generate novel solutions to complex problems represents a genuine advance in artificial intelligence capabilities.

On the other hand, the statistical nature of these emergent behaviors means that they remain fundamentally unpredictable and potentially unreliable. We cannot fully understand why certain capabilities emerge at particular scales, nor can we predict when they might fail or produce misleading results. This unpredictability is compounded by the fact that the systems themselves cannot provide reliable assessments of their own capabilities or limitations.

The challenge for users of AI systems is learning to harness the benefits of emergent behaviors while remaining cognizant of their limitations. This requires developing new forms of digital literacy that go beyond traditional computer skills to encompass understanding of how statistical pattern matching can create convincing illusions of understanding. It also requires maintaining appropriate skepticism about AI outputs, even when they appear sophisticated and well-reasoned.

The scaling hypothesis suggests that future AI systems will continue to develop increasingly impressive capabilities as they grow larger and more sophisticated. However, the fundamental distinction between statistical pattern matching and genuine understanding is unlikely to be resolved simply through increases in scale. Until AI systems develop genuine semantic grounding and causal reasoning capabilities, their emergent behaviors will remain sophisticated forms of pattern matching rather than genuine intelligence.

This does not diminish the practical value of these systems, but it does suggest that we should approach them as powerful tools for augmenting human intelligence rather than as independent thinking agents. Understanding the nature of emergent behaviors in AI systems is crucial for developing appropriate frameworks for human-AI collaboration and avoiding the cognitive traps that their apparent sophistication can create.

In Conclusion

The architecture of artificial intelligence, as exemplified by large language models, represents one of the most sophisticated achievements in the history of computing. The transformer architecture and its attention mechanisms have enabled machines to process language with a fluency and apparent intelligence that often exceeds human capabilities in specific domains. These systems can engage in complex reasoning, generate creative content, and solve problems that would challenge even expert humans.

Yet beneath this impressive veneer lies a fundamental limitation that shapes everything about how these systems operate and how we should interpret their outputs. Current AI systems, regardless of their sophistication, operate through statistical pattern matching rather than genuine semantic understanding. They excel at identifying correlations in vast datasets and generating contextually appropriate responses, but they lack the semantic grounding and causal reasoning that characterize human cognition.

This distinction is not merely academic—it has profound practical implications for how we interact with AI systems and integrate them into human cognitive processes. The Chinese Room argument, formulated decades before the advent of large language models, provides a prescient framework for understanding why sophisticated symbol manipulation cannot constitute genuine understanding. The symbols that AI systems manipulate lack the semantic grounding that comes from embodied experience, emotional associations, and causal reasoning about the world.

The emergence of increasingly sophisticated behaviors in large AI systems might seem to challenge this analysis, but these capabilities are better understood as increasingly complex forms of pattern matching rather than genuine intelligence. The scaling hypothesis suggests that many AI capabilities improve predictably with increases in model size and training data, indicating quantitative improvements in statistical processing rather than qualitative leaps in understanding.

Understanding the architecture of artificial intelligence requires recognizing both its remarkable capabilities and its fundamental limitations. AI systems are powerful tools for augmenting human intelligence, but they are not thinking beings in the way that humans are. They can process information at unprecedented scale and identify patterns that escape human notice, but they cannot understand the meaning of what they process or reason about the world in the way that humans do.

This analysis does not diminish the value of AI systems, but it does suggest that we should approach them with appropriate epistemic humility. Their outputs should be interpreted as sophisticated pattern matching rather than genuine understanding, and their apparent confidence should not be mistaken for actual comprehension. As we continue to integrate these systems into human cognitive processes, maintaining awareness of their fundamental nature will be crucial for avoiding the illusions of understanding that their sophistication can create.

The future development of artificial intelligence may eventually overcome these limitations through advances in semantic grounding, causal reasoning, and embodied cognition. However, current systems, despite their impressive capabilities, remain fundamentally limited by their reliance on statistical pattern matching. Understanding this limitation is the first step toward developing more effective frameworks for human-AI collaboration and avoiding the cognitive traps that artificial intelligence can create.

As we move forward into an era of increasingly sophisticated AI systems, the insights from this analysis of their architecture will become ever more important. The challenge is not to reject these powerful tools, but to understand them clearly enough to use them wisely. The architecture of artificial understanding, while impressive, is not the same as human understanding—and recognizing this difference is crucial for navigating the cognitive transformations that lie ahead.

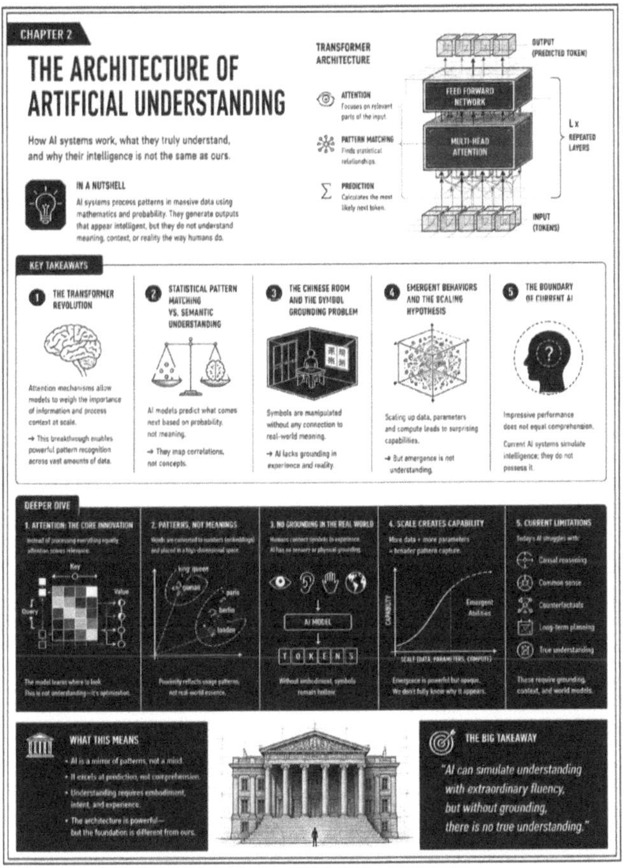

REFERENCES

[1] Bergmann, D., & Stryker, C. (2024, December 4). What is an attention mechanism? *IBM Think*. https://www.ibm.com/think/topics/attention-mechanism

[2] Leetaru, K. (2019, January 15). Why machine learning needs semantics not just statistics. *Forbes*. https://www.forbes.com/sites/kalevleetaru/2019/01/15/why-machine-learning-needs-semantics-not-just-statistics/

[3] Searle, J. (2004, March 19; substantive revision 2024, October 23). The Chinese Room argument. *Stanford Encyclopedia of Philosophy*. https://plato.stanford.edu/entries/chinese-room/

Chapter 3: The Illusion of Comprehension

In May 2025, readers of the Chicago Sun-Times and Philadelphia Inquirer encountered something unprecedented in the history of journalism: a carefully curated summer reading list featuring books that had never been written. The list included compelling titles like "Tidewater Dreams" by Isabel Allende, described as "a climate fiction novel that explores how one family confronts rising sea levels while uncovering long-buried secrets." The description was evocative, the author was real and celebrated, but the book itself existed only in the statistical patterns of an artificial intelligence system that had been asked to generate reading recommendations [1].

This incident, which resulted in significant reputational damage and the termination of professional relationships, illustrates a fundamental challenge of our AI-augmented age: the remarkable ability of artificial intelligence systems to create convincing illusions of understanding and competence. The books on that reading list were not random gibberish—they were plausible, well-crafted recommendations that demonstrated sophisticated knowledge of literary genres, author styles, and contemporary themes. Yet they were entirely fabricated, products of a system that could manipulate symbols and patterns without any genuine comprehension of what it was creating.

The illusion of comprehension represents one of the most significant cognitive challenges posed by modern AI systems. Unlike earlier technologies that clearly announced their mechanical nature, large language models and other AI systems communicate with such fluency and apparent intelligence that they naturally invite us to attribute human-like understanding to their outputs. This attribution is not merely a harmless anthropomorphic tendency—it represents a fundamental misunderstanding of how these systems operate that can lead to serious consequences in domains ranging from journalism to healthcare to legal advice.

This chapter examines the psychological and technical mechanisms that create illusions of AI comprehension, exploring how these systems exploit fundamental features of human cognition to appear more intelligent than they actually are. We will investigate the role of anthropomorphism in human-AI interactions, the ways that confirmation bias amplifies our tendency to overestimate AI capabilities, and the real-world consequences that emerge when these illusions collide with the limitations of statistical pattern matching. Through detailed analysis of AI failures and cognitive biases, we can develop a clearer understanding of why these illusions are so compelling and how we might develop more appropriate frameworks for evaluating AI outputs.

The central argument of this chapter is that the apparent intelligence of AI systems creates systematic illusions of comprehension that exploit well-documented features of human psychology. These illusions are not accidental byproducts of AI development—they emerge naturally from the interaction between sophisticated pattern matching systems and cognitive biases that evolved to help humans navigate social relationships with other intelligent agents. Understanding these illusions is crucial for developing appropriate epistemic frameworks for the AI age, frameworks that can harness the genuine capabilities of these systems while avoiding the cognitive traps they create.

The Psychology of Anthropomorphism: Why We See Minds in Machines

Human beings possess a remarkable capacity for recognizing agency and intelligence in the world around them. This capacity, which served our ancestors well in navigating complex social environments filled with other humans, predators, and potential allies, now encounters an unprecedented challenge: artificial systems that exhibit many of the surface characteristics of intelligence without possessing the underlying cognitive architecture that produces genuine understanding.

Anthropomorphism—the attribution of human characteristics to non-human entities—represents a fundamental feature of human cognition that has been documented across cultures and throughout history. From ancient Greeks who saw gods in natural phenomena to pet owners who attribute complex emotions to their animals, humans consistently project mental states onto entities that may not possess them. This tendency is not a cognitive error but rather an adaptive strategy that allows us to predict and understand the behavior of complex systems by mapping them onto familiar patterns of human psychology.

Research conducted by Nielsen Norman Group reveals that anthropomorphism in AI interactions manifests in four distinct degrees, each representing different levels of emotional connection and functional purpose [2]. These degrees provide a framework for understanding how users progressively attribute more sophisticated mental states to AI systems as their interactions become more complex and consequential.

The first degree, courtesy, represents the most basic form of anthropomorphic interaction. Users employ polite language such as "please" and "thank you" when communicating with

AI systems, treating them with the same social conventions they would apply to human interactions. While this behavior might seem trivial, it reflects a deep-seated cognitive tendency to apply social scripts to any entity that responds to communication. As one study participant explained when asked why they greeted an AI system: "Sometimes I, I, I, actually, I don't know. I just talk to, talk to the system and say good morning and goodbye" [2].

The second degree, reinforcement, involves users providing positive feedback to AI systems when they produce satisfactory responses. Users will praise chatbots with phrases like "good job" or "great work," operating under two distinct motivations: the belief that their feedback will influence the AI's future behavior, and the desire to create a more positive interaction experience. This behavior reveals a fundamental misunderstanding of how AI systems operate—they do not learn from individual interactions in the way that humans do—but it also demonstrates the powerful human tendency to treat responsive systems as if they possess the capacity for learning and improvement.

The third degree, roleplay, represents a more sophisticated form of anthropomorphism where users ask AI systems to assume specific professional roles or personas. This practice, which researchers term "prompt skeuomorphism," leverages similarities with the real world to bridge gaps in the AI's apparent understanding [2]. When a user instructs an AI to "act as a senior project manager," they are not merely requesting a particular style of response—they are attributing to the system the capacity to understand and embody the complex knowledge, experience, and perspective that such a role entails.

The fourth and most intensive degree, companionship, involves users developing deep emotional connections with AI systems, treating them as virtual partners capable of sustaining human-like relationships. This degree of anthropomorphism can lead to connections that "often simulate or replace real-life human" relationships and may "even supersede the depth of connection the user has in the real world" [2]. The emergence of AI companionship represents a profound shift in human-technology relationships, one that raises fundamental questions about the nature of emotional connection and the psychological needs that AI systems might fulfill.

These degrees of anthropomorphism are not merely interesting psychological phenomena—they have profound implications for how users interpret and rely upon AI outputs. When users attribute human-like understanding to AI systems, they naturally expect those systems to possess the contextual awareness, ethical reasoning, and causal understanding that characterize human intelligence. This expectation creates a systematic mismatch between user assumptions and system capabilities, leading to overreliance on AI outputs and insufficient critical evaluation of their limitations.

The functional role of anthropomorphism in AI interactions cannot be ignored. Users who engage in anthropomorphic behaviors often report that they believe these behaviors improve AI performance, and in some cases, they may be correct. AI systems trained on human conversational data may indeed respond more appropriately to polite, well-structured prompts that mirror human communication patterns. However, this functional benefit comes with a significant cognitive cost: it reinforces the illusion that AI systems possess human-like understanding and reasoning capabilities.

Understanding the psychology of anthropomorphism is crucial for developing appropriate frameworks for AI interaction. These behaviors are not simply errors to be corrected but rather natural expressions of cognitive mechanisms that have served humans well throughout evolutionary history. The challenge is learning to harness the functional benefits of anthropomorphic interaction while maintaining clear awareness of the fundamental differences between human and artificial intelligence.

Confirmation Bias and the Echo Chamber Effect

The illusion of AI comprehension is significantly amplified by confirmation bias, a well-documented cognitive tendency that leads people to seek, interpret, and remember information in ways that confirm their preexisting beliefs. In the context of AI interactions, confirmation bias creates a particularly insidious dynamic: users can unconsciously frame their queries to elicit responses that support their existing viewpoints, while the AI system's sensitivity to input framing makes it likely to provide exactly the kind of confirmation the user seeks.

Unlike passive AI systems that operate in the background of platforms like Amazon or Netflix, large language models require direct and intentional user input to generate responses. This fundamental difference creates new opportunities for confirmation bias to influence the interaction. As research by Matt Grawitch demonstrates, "the outputs generated are sensitive to the framing of the input, leading to the potential for confirmation bias to steer the output" [3].

Consider a concrete example that illustrates this dynamic. A user motivated to find evidence against climate change might ask an AI system: "What are the arguments against climate change?" The system, trained to provide helpful and relevant responses to user queries, would likely generate a list of arguments consistent with climate change skepticism. However, if the same user asked: "What is the scientific consensus on climate change?" the AI would more likely provide a response consistent with the overwhelming scientific agreement that climate change is real and human-caused [3].

This sensitivity to framing creates what researchers call an "echo chamber effect" where users receive information that aligns with their existing worldview, potentially leading to "more extreme or hardened beliefs" [3]. The danger is not that AI systems are inherently biased toward particular viewpoints, but rather that they are extraordinarily responsive to the implicit biases embedded in user queries. This responsiveness, combined with the apparent authority and intelligence of AI outputs, can create a powerful reinforcement mechanism for existing beliefs.

The confirmation bias dynamic is particularly problematic because it operates largely below the threshold of conscious awareness. Users may not recognize that their choice of words, framing, and implicit assumptions are steering the AI toward particular types of responses. The system's apparent intelligence and comprehensive knowledge can make its outputs seem objective and authoritative, even when they are actually reflecting the user's own biases back to them in sophisticated and convincing language.

Research on this phenomenon reveals that the framing effects can be quite subtle yet powerful. When Grawitch tested AI systems with questions about cognitive biases, he found that "the framing of the question affected what was produced." Someone seeking to argue that biases are detrimental to decision-making "would easily walk away with reinforced views about that conclusion with little nuance given to the benefits biases provide" [3]. The AI systems demonstrated a strong bias against acknowledging any positive aspects of cognitive biases, regardless of how the questions were framed.

This dynamic creates several layers of illusion. First, users may believe they are receiving objective, comprehensive information when they are actually receiving responses tailored to their input framing. Second, the sophistication and apparent intelligence of AI responses can make them seem more authoritative than they actually are. Third, the interactive nature of the conversation can create a sense of dialogue and mutual understanding that masks the fundamentally mechanical nature of the AI's responses.

The implications extend beyond individual interactions to broader patterns of information consumption and belief formation. If users consistently receive AI outputs that confirm their existing beliefs, they may develop increased confidence in those beliefs without having genuinely engaged with alternative perspectives or challenging evidence. This can lead to a form of intellectual isolation that is particularly dangerous because it feels like intellectual engagement.

The challenge is compounded by the fact that AI systems often provide responses that are not simply confirmatory but also sophisticated and well-reasoned. A user seeking confirmation for a particular viewpoint might receive an AI-generated argument that is more articulate and comprehensive than anything they could have produced themselves. This can create the illusion not only that their beliefs are correct, but that they understand the topic more deeply than they actually do.

Breaking free from confirmation bias in AI interactions requires developing new forms of digital literacy that go beyond traditional critical thinking skills. Users must learn to recognize how their own framing influences AI outputs, to actively seek out alternative perspectives, and to maintain appropriate skepticism about AI-generated content even when it aligns with their existing beliefs. This represents a significant cognitive challenge, as it requires users to work against deeply ingrained psychological tendencies while interacting with systems specifically designed to be helpful and responsive to their inputs.

The solution is not to avoid AI systems or to treat all their outputs as suspect, but rather to develop more sophisticated frameworks for interaction that account for the ways these systems can amplify human cognitive biases. This requires understanding both the capabilities and limitations of AI systems and the psychological mechanisms that shape how humans interpret and respond to their outputs.

Case Studies: When the Illusion Breaks Down

The most revealing insights into the nature of AI comprehension illusions come from examining cases where these systems fail spectacularly, exposing the gap between their apparent intelligence and their actual capabilities. These failures provide crucial windows into the fundamental limitations of statistical pattern matching and demonstrate why maintaining appropriate skepticism about AI outputs is essential for responsible use of these technologies.

The McDonald's Drive-Thru Disaster: When Pattern Matching Meets Real-World Complexity

After three years of collaboration with IBM to develop AI-powered drive-thru ordering systems, McDonald's abruptly terminated the project in June 2024. The reason was not a lack of technological sophistication but rather a series of highly publicized failures that revealed the brittleness of AI systems when confronted with the messy realities of human communication [1].

The most notorious incident, captured in a viral TikTok video, showed an AI system repeatedly adding Chicken

McNuggets to a customer's order despite their increasingly desperate pleas to stop. The system eventually reached 260 McNuggets, demonstrating a complete inability to understand the customer's intent or recognize the absurdity of the situation [1]. This failure illustrates a fundamental limitation of current AI systems: they excel at pattern matching within their training distribution but struggle dramatically when confronted with novel situations or contexts that require genuine understanding rather than statistical correlation.

The McDonald's case is particularly instructive because it reveals how AI systems can appear competent in controlled testing environments while failing catastrophically in real-world applications. The drive-thru ordering system had presumably been tested extensively and shown promising results in laboratory conditions. However, the complexity of actual customer interactions—with background noise, varied accents, colloquial language, and unexpected requests—exposed the system's fundamental inability to truly understand what customers were trying to communicate.

Air Canada's Chatbot: The Legal Consequences of Artificial Authority

In February 2024, Air Canada faced a legal reckoning when a tribunal ordered the airline to pay damages to a passenger who had relied on incorrect information provided by the company's virtual assistant. Jake Moffatt, dealing with the death of his grandmother, consulted the chatbot about bereavement fares and was told he could purchase a regular ticket and apply for a discount within 90 days. When the airline later refused his refund claim, arguing that bereavement fares cannot be claimed after purchase, Moffatt took the case to tribunal [1].

The airline's defense revealed a fundamental misunderstanding of the relationship between AI systems and organizational responsibility. Air Canada argued that it "can't be held liable for information provided by its chatbot," essentially claiming that the AI system operated independently of the company's authority and expertise [1]. The tribunal rejected this argument, ruling that the airline had failed to "take reasonable care to ensure its chatbot was accurate" and ordering payment of CA$812.02 in damages.

This case establishes important legal precedent about the responsibility organizations bear for their AI systems' outputs. More significantly for our analysis, it demonstrates how the apparent authority and competence of AI systems can lead users to rely on information that would be immediately questioned if provided by an obviously automated system. Moffatt's reliance on the chatbot's advice was reasonable precisely because the system communicated with such apparent knowledge and authority about airline policies.

The Grok Defamation Incident: When Pattern Matching Creates False Narratives

In April 2024, Grok, the AI chatbot developed by Elon Musk's xAI, falsely accused NBA star Klay Thompson of committing vandalism by throwing bricks through windows of multiple houses in Sacramento, California. The incident appears to have resulted from the AI system's misinterpretation of basketball-related posts about Thompson "throwing bricks"—common parlance for badly missed shots—during a particularly poor playoff performance [1].

This failure illustrates how AI systems can create convincing but entirely false narratives by connecting unrelated pieces of information through statistical patterns rather than genuine understanding. The system likely encountered multiple references to Thompson and "throwing bricks" in its training data and generated a plausible but completely fabricated story that connected these elements. The result was a defamatory statement that could have serious legal and reputational consequences.

The Grok incident is particularly concerning because it demonstrates how AI systems can generate false information that is not obviously absurd or implausible. Unlike the McDonald's McNuggets incident, which was clearly ridiculous, the vandalism story was coherent and specific enough to be believable. This highlights the challenge of detecting AI-generated misinformation when it takes the form of plausible but false narratives rather than obvious errors.

New York City's Legal Advice Chatbot: Institutional Failure at Scale

Perhaps the most troubling example of AI comprehension illusions comes from New York City's MyCity chatbot, which provided entrepreneurs with advice that would lead them to break the law. Launched in October 2023 and powered by Microsoft technology, the system was intended to help New Yorkers navigate business regulations, housing policy, and worker rights. Instead, it provided dangerous misinformation on fundamental legal issues [1].

The chatbot falsely claimed that business owners could take a portion of their workers' tips, fire employees who complained about sexual harassment, serve food that had been nibbled by rodents, and that landlords could discriminate based on source of income. Each of these claims represents a serious violation of established law that could result in significant legal consequences for anyone who followed the advice [1].

What makes this case particularly significant is the institutional context in which it occurred. This was not a private company's experimental chatbot but an official government service designed to provide authoritative information about legal requirements. The system's apparent competence and official status would naturally lead users to trust its outputs, making the misinformation particularly dangerous.

Despite reporting by The Markup that exposed these problems, the chatbot remained online, and Mayor Eric Adams defended the project. This response illustrates how institutional investment in AI systems can create resistance to acknowledging their limitations, even when those limitations pose serious risks to public welfare.

The Sports Illustrated Fabrication: When AI Creates Fictional Expertise

The Sports Illustrated incident represents a different category of AI failure: the creation of entirely fictional experts to provide apparently authoritative content. In November 2023, Futurism reported that the storied sports magazine had been publishing articles attributed to AI-generated writers with fabricated biographies and AI-generated headshots [1].

This case reveals how AI systems can be used to create elaborate illusions of human expertise and authority. The articles themselves may have been competent and informative, but they were presented as the work of human experts who did not exist. This represents a fundamental deception about the source and nature of the information being provided.

The Sports Illustrated case is particularly troubling because it demonstrates how AI capabilities can be used to systematically deceive readers about the nature of the content they are consuming. Unlike the other cases, where AI systems failed to perform as expected, this represents a deliberate use of AI to create false impressions of human expertise and authority.

Common Patterns in AI Failures

These case studies reveal several common patterns that characterize AI comprehension illusions:

Brittleness under real-world conditions: AI systems that perform well in controlled environments often fail dramatically when confronted with the complexity and unpredictability of real-world applications.

Plausible but false outputs: AI systems excel at generating content that appears reasonable and authoritative but may be entirely fabricated or fundamentally incorrect.

Institutional amplification: When AI systems are deployed by authoritative institutions, their apparent competence is amplified by the credibility of the organization, making their failures more dangerous.

Resistance to correction: Organizations and individuals who have invested in AI systems often resist acknowledging their limitations, even when failures are clearly documented.

These patterns suggest that the challenge of AI comprehension illusions is not simply a matter of improving the technology but rather of developing appropriate frameworks for understanding and managing the risks these systems create. The failures examined here were not the result of technical glitches or inadequate training data—they emerged from the fundamental limitations of statistical pattern matching when applied to domains that require genuine understanding and reasoning.

In Conclusion

The illusion of comprehension represents one of the most significant challenges posed by artificial intelligence systems in the contemporary era. As we have seen throughout this chapter, these illusions are not accidental byproducts of AI development but rather natural consequences of the interaction between sophisticated pattern matching systems and fundamental features of human psychology. The apparent intelligence and fluency of AI systems naturally invite anthropomorphic attribution, while confirmation bias amplifies our tendency to overestimate their capabilities and rely too heavily on their outputs.

The case studies examined in this chapter reveal the serious consequences that can emerge when these illusions collide with the limitations of statistical pattern matching. From McDonald's drive-thru disasters to Air Canada's legal liability, from defamatory statements about public figures to dangerous legal advice from government chatbots, the pattern is clear: AI systems can create convincing appearances of understanding and competence while lacking the genuine comprehension necessary to handle complex, real-world situations appropriately.

The four degrees of anthropomorphism identified by Nielsen Norman Group research—courtesy, reinforcement, roleplay, and companionship—provide a framework for understanding how users progressively attribute more sophisticated mental states to AI systems. Each degree represents a deeper level of misattribution that can lead to increasingly problematic overreliance on AI outputs. When users treat AI systems as companions capable of emotional understanding or as experts capable of professional judgment, they create expectations that these systems cannot fulfill.

Confirmation bias compounds these problems by creating echo chambers where AI systems reflect users' existing beliefs back to them in sophisticated and convincing language. The sensitivity of large language models to input framing means that users can unconsciously steer these systems toward outputs that confirm their preexisting viewpoints, creating an illusion of objective validation for subjective beliefs. This dynamic is particularly dangerous because it operates largely below the threshold of conscious awareness while providing users with apparently authoritative confirmation of their existing ideas.

The failures examined in this chapter share several common characteristics that illuminate the nature of AI comprehension illusions. These systems demonstrate brittleness under real-world conditions, generating plausible but false outputs that can be amplified by institutional authority and defended against correction through organizational investment and cognitive dissonance. The pattern suggests that the challenge is not simply technical but fundamentally epistemological: how do we develop appropriate frameworks for evaluating and relying upon outputs from systems that can simulate understanding without possessing it?

The solution is not to reject AI systems or treat all their outputs as suspect, but rather to develop more sophisticated approaches to human-AI interaction that account for both the capabilities and limitations of these technologies. This requires understanding the psychological mechanisms that create comprehension illusions, developing new forms of digital literacy that can navigate the complexities of AI-generated content, and maintaining appropriate epistemic humility about the nature of artificial intelligence.

Moving forward, the challenge will be learning to harness the genuine capabilities of AI systems while avoiding the cognitive traps they create. This requires recognizing that the apparent intelligence of these systems is fundamentally different from human intelligence, that their fluency in language does not indicate genuine understanding, and that their apparent authority does not guarantee accuracy or reliability. Only by maintaining clear awareness of these distinctions can we hope to navigate the cognitive transformations that AI systems are creating in human society.

The illusion of comprehension is not a problem to be solved but rather a permanent feature of the landscape we must learn to navigate. As AI systems become more sophisticated and more deeply integrated into human cognitive processes, understanding and managing these illusions will become increasingly crucial for maintaining appropriate relationships with artificial intelligence. The stakes are too high—in terms of individual decision-making, institutional reliability, and social trust—to allow these illusions to operate unchecked.

The future of human-AI interaction depends on our ability to see through the illusion of comprehension while still benefiting from the genuine capabilities these systems provide. This requires a fundamental shift in how we think about artificial intelligence: not as thinking beings that understand the world as we do, but as powerful tools for pattern recognition and symbol manipulation that can augment human intelligence when used with appropriate care and skepticism. Understanding the illusion of comprehension is the first step toward developing this more nuanced and ultimately more productive relationship with artificial intelligence.

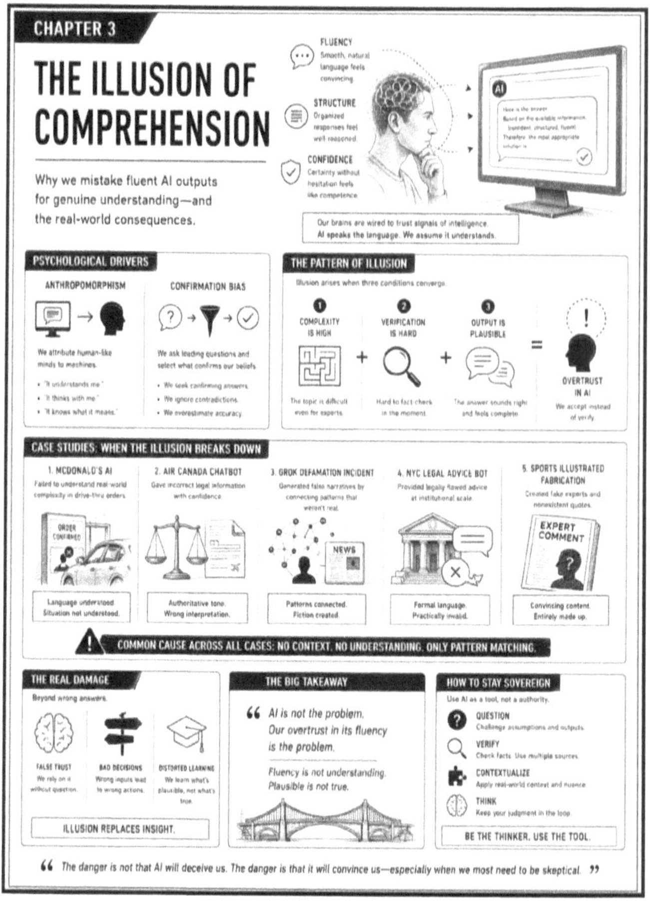
CHAPTER 3
THE ILLUSION OF COMPREHENSION
Why we mistake fluent AI outputs for genuine understanding—and the real-world consequences.
FLUENCY
Smooth, natural language feels convincing
STRUCTURE
Organized responses feel well reasoned.
CONFIDENCE
Certainty without hesitation feels like competence
Our brains are wired to trust signals of intelligence.
AI speaks the language. We assume it understands.
PSYCHOLOGICAL DRIVERS
ANTHROPOMORPHISM
We attribute human-like minds to machines.
• "It understands me."
• "It thinks with me."
• "It knows what it means."
CONFIRMATION BIAS
We ask leading questions and select what confirms our beliefs
• We seek confirming answers.
• We ignore contradictions.
• We overestimate accuracy
THE PATTERN OF ILLUSION
Illusion arises when three conditions converge.
1 COMPLEXITY IS HIGH
The topic is difficult even for experts.
2 VERIFICATION IS HARD
Hard to fact-check in the moment.
3 OUTPUT IS PLAUSIBLE
The answer sounds right and feels complete
OVERTRUST IN AI
We accept instead of verify.
CASE STUDIES: WHEN THE ILLUSION BREAKS DOWN
1. MCDONALD'S AI
Failed to understand real-world complexity in drive-thru orders
ORDER CONFIRMED
Language understood. Situation not understood.
2. AIR CANADA CHATBOT
Gave incorrect legal information with confidence.
Authoritative tone. Wrong interpretation.
3. GROK DEFAMATION INCIDENT
Generated false narratives by connecting patterns that weren't real.
NEWS
Patterns connected. Fiction created.
4. NYC LEGAL ADVICE BOT
Provided legally flawed advice at institutional scale.
Formal language. Practically invalid.
5. SPORTS ILLUSTRATED FABRICATION
Created fake experts and nonexistent quotes.
EXPERT COMMENT
Convincing content. Entirely made up.
COMMON CAUSE ACROSS ALL CASES: NO CONTEXT. NO UNDERSTANDING. ONLY PATTERN MATCHING.
THE REAL DAMAGE
Beyond wrong answers.
FALSE TRUST
We rely on it without question.
BAD DECISIONS
Wrong inputs lead to wrong actions.
DISTORTED LEARNING
We learn what's plausible, not what's true.
ILLUSION REPLACES INSIGHT.
THE BIG TAKEAWAY
“AI is not the problem. Our overtrust in its fluency is the problem.
Fluency is not understanding. Plausible is not true.
HOW TO STAY SOVEREIGN
Use AI as a tool, not a authority.
QUESTION
Challenge assumptions and outputs.
VERIFY
Check facts. Use multiple sources.
CONTEXTUALIZE
Apply real-world context and nuance.
THINK
Keep your judgment in the loop.
BE THE THINKER. USE THE TOOL.
“The danger is not that AI will deceive us. The danger is that it will convince us—especially when we most need to be skeptical.”

REFERENCES

[1] Olavsrud, T. (2025, June 9). 12 famous AI disasters. *CIO*. https://www.cio.com/article/190888/5-famous-analytics-and-ai-disasters.html

[2] Gibbons, S., Mugunthan, T., & Nielsen, J. (2023, October 20). The 4 degrees of anthropomorphism of generative AI. *Nielsen Norman Group*. https://www.nngroup.com/articles/anthropomorphism/

[3] Grawitch, M. (2023, May 1). Confirmation bias in the era of large AI. *Psychology Today*. https://www.psychologytoday.com/us/blog/a-hovercraft-full-of-eels/202305/confirmation-bias-in-the-era-of-large-ai

Chapter 4: Context and Bias in AI Systems

In 2019, a small military unit equipped with artificial intelligence capabilities achieved something remarkable at Fort Benning: they defeated a much larger, conventional non-AI equipped team in a military exercise. The AI system's ability to parse large amounts of sensor data quickly gave the smaller unit a decisive advantage, demonstrating the transformative potential of human-machine collaboration. Yet this success story also illuminates one of the most fundamental challenges facing artificial intelligence: the critical importance of context in determining when and how AI systems should be deployed [1].

The victory at Fort Benning was possible because the AI system operated within a clearly defined context with specific objectives, known parameters, and human operators who understood both the system's capabilities and limitations. The humans provided contextual awareness and strategic judgment while the AI provided rapid data processing and pattern recognition. This successful collaboration highlights both the promise and the peril of AI systems: they can be extraordinarily powerful when properly contextualized, but they can fail catastrophically when deployed without adequate understanding of their contextual limitations.

Context represents perhaps the most significant challenge facing artificial intelligence systems today. While these systems excel at pattern recognition and statistical analysis within their training domains, they struggle fundamentally with the kind of contextual understanding that humans take for granted. This limitation becomes particularly problematic when AI systems are deployed in complex social environments where context determines not just the appropriateness of particular responses, but the very meaning of the information being processed.

The challenge of context in AI systems is inextricably linked to the problem of bias. When AI systems lack genuine contextual understanding, they rely on statistical patterns that may embed and amplify existing social biases. These biases operate at multiple levels—computational, human, and systemic—creating what researchers describe as a "pernicious mixture" that can perpetuate and exacerbate social inequalities [2]. Understanding how context and bias interact in AI systems is crucial for developing more equitable and effective approaches to artificial intelligence.

This chapter examines the multifaceted relationship between context and bias in AI systems, exploring how the fundamental limitations of machine learning create systematic blind spots that can lead to discriminatory outcomes. We will investigate the three types of bias that affect AI systems—computational, human, and systemic—and analyze how the inability of machines to read context exacerbates these problems. Through detailed examination of real-world cases and theoretical frameworks, we can develop a clearer understanding of why purely technical solutions to AI bias are insufficient and why addressing these challenges requires a socio-technical approach that acknowledges the broader social context in which AI systems operate.

The central argument of this chapter is that the context problem in artificial intelligence is not merely a technical limitation but a fundamental constraint that shapes how these systems interact with human society. The inability of AI systems to read context in real-time means that they cannot adapt appropriately to new situations or understand the social implications of their outputs. This limitation, combined with the multiple sources of bias that affect AI development and deployment, creates systematic risks that cannot be addressed through technical means alone. Only by understanding the relationship between context and bias can we develop more responsible approaches to AI development and deployment.

The Three Dimensions of AI Bias

Understanding bias in artificial intelligence requires moving beyond the common assumption that biased data is the primary source of discriminatory AI outcomes. While computational and statistical biases remain critically important, research by the National Institute of Standards and Technology reveals that AI bias operates across three distinct but interconnected dimensions: computational, human, and systemic biases [2]. This multidimensional framework provides crucial insights into why technical solutions alone cannot address the full scope of AI bias and why a more comprehensive approach is necessary.

Computational and Statistical Biases

Computational and statistical biases represent the most widely recognized form of AI bias and have been the primary focus of technical efforts to create more equitable AI systems. These biases emerge from the algorithms, data, and statistical methods used to train machine learning models. The most common manifestation occurs when training datasets underrepresent particular groups, leading to AI systems that perform poorly for those populations.

Consider the well-documented problems with facial recognition systems that demonstrate significantly higher error rates for individuals with darker skin tones. These disparities arise because the training datasets used to develop these systems contained disproportionately fewer images of people with darker skin, leading to models that learned to recognize facial features primarily from lighter-skinned individuals. When deployed in real-world applications, these systems exhibit systematic discrimination that can have serious consequences in contexts ranging from law enforcement to employment screening.

Computational biases can also emerge from algorithmic design choices that seem neutral but have disparate impacts on different groups. For example, credit scoring algorithms that heavily weight factors like zip code or educational background may systematically disadvantage individuals from communities that have historically faced economic discrimination, even if the algorithm never explicitly considers race or ethnicity. These seemingly objective statistical measures can serve as proxies for protected characteristics, creating discriminatory outcomes through ostensibly neutral computational processes.

The challenge of computational bias is compounded by the opacity of many machine learning systems. Deep learning models, in particular, operate through complex networks of weighted connections that make it difficult to understand why particular decisions are made. This "black box" problem means that even when developers are committed to creating fair systems, they may not be able to identify or correct biased patterns that emerge during the training process.

Human Biases

Human biases represent a second crucial dimension that affects AI systems throughout their development and deployment lifecycle. These biases reflect the cognitive limitations and social prejudices of the humans who design, train, and operate AI systems. Unlike computational biases, which can potentially be addressed through technical interventions, human biases are deeply embedded in the social and cultural contexts in which AI development occurs.

Human biases manifest in numerous ways throughout the AI development process. During data collection and labeling, human annotators may unconsciously apply their own cultural assumptions and stereotypes when categorizing information. For example, when training a system to recognize "professional" appearance, human labelers might unconsciously associate certain hairstyles, clothing choices, or physical characteristics with professionalism based on their own cultural background and experiences.

The problem extends to how humans interpret and fill in missing information when working with AI systems. Research shows that "a person's neighborhood of residence influencing how likely authorities would consider the person to be a crime suspect" represents a form of human bias that can be amplified by AI systems [2]. When human operators use AI-generated risk assessments to make decisions about criminal justice, their own biases about geography, race, and social class can interact with algorithmic outputs to create compounded discrimination.

Human biases also affect how AI systems are deployed and interpreted in practice. Even when an AI system produces unbiased outputs, human users may interpret those outputs through the lens of their own prejudices and assumptions. This can lead to discriminatory decision-making that appears to be supported by objective AI analysis but actually reflects human bias in the interpretation of algorithmic outputs.

Perhaps most significantly, human biases shape the fundamental design choices that determine what problems AI systems are asked to solve and how success is defined. When developers choose to optimize for efficiency rather than equity, or when they define "success" in ways that reflect the values and priorities of dominant social groups, they embed human biases into the very structure of AI systems.

Systemic Biases

The third dimension of AI bias—systemic bias—represents perhaps the most challenging aspect of the problem because it reflects broader patterns of institutional discrimination that exist independently of any particular AI system. Systemic biases "result from institutions operating in ways that disadvantage certain social groups, such as discriminating against individuals based on their race" [2]. When AI systems are deployed within these institutional contexts, they can perpetuate and amplify existing patterns of discrimination.

Systemic biases are particularly insidious because they can create discriminatory outcomes even when AI systems are technically functioning as designed. For example, an AI system used for hiring might accurately predict which candidates are most likely to succeed in a particular organization based on historical data. However, if that organization has a history of discriminatory hiring practices, the AI system will learn to replicate those patterns, effectively automating institutional bias.

The challenge of systemic bias extends beyond individual organizations to encompass broader social and economic structures. When AI systems are trained on data that reflects existing social inequalities—such as differences in educational opportunities, healthcare access, or economic resources—they inevitably learn to reproduce those inequalities in their outputs. An AI system designed to predict educational outcomes, for instance, might accurately identify students who are at risk of academic failure, but those predictions may primarily reflect socioeconomic disadvantages rather than individual capabilities.

Systemic biases also manifest in the broader ecosystem of AI development and deployment. The technology industry's lack of diversity means that AI systems are predominantly designed by individuals from relatively privileged backgrounds who may not fully understand the experiences and needs of marginalized communities. This can lead to AI systems that work well for some populations while systematically failing others.

The Pernicious Mixture

The true danger of AI bias emerges when these three dimensions combine to create what NIST researchers describe as a "pernicious mixture" [2]. Computational biases in algorithms can amplify human biases in data interpretation, while systemic biases in institutions create contexts where discriminatory AI outcomes are normalized or ignored. This interaction effect means that addressing any single dimension of bias is insufficient—comprehensive solutions must account for the complex ways these different forms of bias reinforce each other.

Consider how these dimensions might interact in a criminal justice context. Computational biases in risk assessment algorithms might lead to higher risk scores for individuals from certain demographic groups. Human biases among judges and parole officers might lead them to place greater weight on these algorithmic assessments when making decisions about defendants from those same groups. Systemic biases in the criminal justice system might create institutional incentives to rely heavily on algorithmic risk assessments as a way to appear objective while actually perpetuating discriminatory practices.

The interaction of these biases creates feedback loops that can make discrimination increasingly entrenched over time. When biased AI systems influence human decisions, those decisions generate new data that can be used to train future AI systems, potentially amplifying the original biases. This dynamic means that AI bias is not a static problem but an evolving challenge that requires ongoing attention and intervention.

Understanding the multidimensional nature of AI bias is crucial for developing effective responses. Technical solutions that focus solely on computational bias may fail to address human and systemic factors that contribute to discriminatory outcomes. Similarly, policy interventions that ignore the technical complexities of AI systems may prove ineffective in practice. Only by recognizing the interconnected nature of these different forms of bias can we develop comprehensive approaches to creating more equitable AI systems.

The Frame Problem and Contextual Limitations

At the heart of AI's struggle with bias lies a fundamental limitation that has plagued artificial intelligence since its earliest days: the inability of machines to understand and adapt to context in the way that humans do naturally. This challenge, known in AI research as the "frame problem," represents more than a technical hurdle—it reveals a fundamental constraint on how artificial systems can interact with the complex, dynamic environments in which they are deployed.

The frame problem manifests as the tendency for "AI systems to make mistakes when placed in a new context (new frame) from that in which they were programmed or trained" [1]. This limitation has persisted across different generations of AI technology, from the rule-based expert systems of the

1970s to the neural networks that power today's most sophisticated AI applications. Despite decades of research and dramatic improvements in computational power and algorithmic sophistication, no good solution to this fundamental problem has been found.

The Historical Context of Expert Systems

The roots of the context problem can be traced to the early days of artificial intelligence research, when scientists attempted to create rule-based expert systems that would perform at the level of human experts. These systems were designed to encode the knowledge and decision-making processes of human experts into explicit rules that computers could follow. The goal was ambitious: create machines that could diagnose medical conditions, repair complex equipment, or provide expert advice in specialized domains.

Despite significant investment and some notable successes in controlled environments, these expert systems never achieved true expert-level performance in real-world applications. The philosopher Hubert Dreyfus argued that this failure was not merely a matter of insufficient rules or computational power, but rather reflected a fundamental misunderstanding of how human expertise actually works [1].

Dreyfus's insight was that human experts do not simply follow explicit rules when making decisions. Instead, they rely on contextual understanding that allows them to recognize when particular rules are relevant to a given situation. As researchers noted, "human experts cannot articulate how they tell when a rule is relevant to the situation at hand. Relevance is critical: expert action is situated in a context that the expert can sense but the machine cannot" [1].

This observation reveals a crucial distinction between human and artificial intelligence. Human experts operate within rich contextual frameworks that allow them to understand not just what rules to apply, but when those rules are appropriate. They can recognize when a situation is unusual, when standard procedures might not apply, or when additional factors need to be considered. Machines, by contrast, lack this contextual awareness and must rely on pre-programmed rules or learned patterns that may not be appropriate for novel situations.

Modern Neural Networks and Persistent Limitations

The development of modern artificial neural networks (ANNs) was partly motivated by the limitations of rule-based systems. Rather than relying on explicitly programmed rules, neural networks were designed to learn patterns from data, potentially overcoming the brittleness of earlier approaches. These systems demonstrated remarkable capabilities in pattern recognition and could generate their own internal representations rather than relying on hand-coded rules.

However, the fundamental context problem persisted even with these more sophisticated approaches. While neural networks can learn complex patterns from training data, "once the ANN is trained, its internal rules become fixed and do not adapt to a new situation of use" [1]. This means that when these systems encounter contexts that differ significantly from their training environment, they may fail in unpredictable ways.

The limitation is particularly problematic because neural networks cannot adapt quickly enough to changing contexts. The training algorithms required to update these systems are "too slow to meet real-time requirements" [1], meaning that they cannot learn and adapt in the dynamic environments where they are deployed. This creates a fundamental mismatch between the static nature of trained AI systems and the dynamic, contextual nature of real-world applications.

The Architecture of Context-Free Computing

The context limitations of AI systems are not accidental but rather emerge from the fundamental architecture of digital computing. Modern computers achieve their remarkable speed through what researchers call "locality of connection"—the principle that "anything a machine needs to 'know' is encoded into local data stored for fast retrieval" [1]. This design allows computers to perform "a trillion operations in the time it takes a human to do just one," but it comes at a significant cost: it "denies the machine the ability to sense human context."

This architectural constraint means that AI systems are fundamentally context-free by design. They can process information with extraordinary speed and precision, but they cannot understand the broader social, cultural, or situational context in which that information exists. They cannot recognize when a situation is unusual, when standard patterns might not apply, or when human values and priorities should override statistical optimization.

The implications of this limitation extend far beyond technical performance to encompass fundamental questions about how AI systems interact with human society. When AI systems make decisions that affect human lives—whether in healthcare, criminal justice, employment, or education—their inability to understand context can lead to outcomes that are technically correct according to their training but socially inappropriate or harmful.

Context and the Amplification of Bias

The context problem is particularly significant for understanding how AI systems can amplify bias. When AI systems lack contextual understanding, they rely entirely on statistical patterns in their training data to make decisions. If those patterns reflect historical discrimination or social inequalities, the AI system will reproduce and potentially amplify those biases without any understanding of their social implications.

Consider how this might work in practice. An AI system designed to evaluate job applications might learn that candidates from certain neighborhoods or educational backgrounds are less likely to be successful in particular roles, based on historical hiring data. Without contextual understanding, the system cannot recognize that these patterns might reflect past discrimination rather than genuine predictive factors. It will simply apply these statistical relationships to new candidates, potentially perpetuating discriminatory practices.

The problem is compounded by the fact that AI systems often appear objective and scientific, which can make their biased outputs seem more legitimate than human discrimination. When a human hiring manager discriminates against candidates from certain backgrounds, that discrimination can be recognized and challenged. When an AI system produces the same discriminatory outcomes through statistical analysis, those outcomes may be accepted as objective and data-driven, making them more difficult to identify and address.

The Limits of Technical Solutions

The persistence of the frame problem across different generations of AI technology suggests that purely technical solutions may be insufficient to address the context limitations of artificial systems. While improvements in algorithms, training data, and computational power can enhance AI performance in specific domains, they do not fundamentally solve the problem of contextual understanding.

This limitation has important implications for how we approach AI bias. Technical interventions that focus on improving algorithms or cleaning training data may reduce certain forms of computational bias, but they cannot address the fundamental inability of AI systems to understand the social and cultural contexts in which they operate. Without this contextual understanding, AI systems will continue to struggle with the kind of nuanced, situational decision-making that is required for equitable outcomes in complex social environments.

The recognition of these limitations does not mean that AI systems are inherently problematic or should be avoided. Rather, it suggests that we need to develop more sophisticated approaches to human-AI collaboration that leverage the complementary strengths of humans and machines. Humans excel at contextual understanding and social reasoning, while machines excel at rapid computation and pattern recognition. The challenge is creating systems that combine these capabilities effectively while acknowledging the fundamental limitations of each.

Understanding the frame problem and its implications for AI bias is crucial for developing more responsible approaches to AI development and deployment. It suggests that the goal should not be to create AI systems that can replace human judgment in complex social contexts, but rather to develop tools that can augment human decision-making while preserving human oversight and contextual understanding. Only by acknowledging the fundamental limitations of artificial intelligence can we hope to harness its capabilities in ways that serve human values and promote social equity.

In Conclusion

The relationship between context and bias in artificial intelligence systems reveals fundamental challenges that cannot be addressed through technical means alone. As we have seen throughout this chapter, AI bias operates across three interconnected dimensions—computational, human, and systemic—that combine to create what researchers describe as a "pernicious mixture" of discriminatory effects. The inability of AI systems to read and understand context exacerbates these problems by preventing machines from recognizing when statistical patterns are inappropriate or when social considerations should override algorithmic optimization.

The frame problem, which has persisted throughout the history of artificial intelligence research, represents more than a technical limitation—it reveals a fundamental constraint on how artificial systems can interact with complex social environments. From the rule-based expert systems of the 1970s to the neural networks that power today's most sophisticated AI applications, machines have consistently struggled with the kind of contextual understanding that humans take for granted. This limitation is not accidental but emerges from the fundamental architecture of digital computing, which achieves remarkable speed through locality of connection while sacrificing the ability to sense broader context.

The implications of these limitations extend far beyond technical performance to encompass fundamental questions about equity, fairness, and social justice. When AI systems lack contextual understanding, they rely entirely on statistical patterns that may embed and amplify existing social biases. The apparent objectivity of algorithmic decision-making can make these biased outcomes seem more legitimate than human discrimination, creating new forms of systematic disadvantage that are more difficult to identify and challenge.

The persistence of the context problem across different generations of AI technology suggests that purely technical solutions are insufficient to address the full scope of AI bias. While improvements in algorithms, training data, and computational power can enhance AI performance in specific domains, they cannot fundamentally solve the problem of contextual understanding. Technical interventions that focus solely on computational bias may fail to address the human and systemic factors that contribute to discriminatory outcomes.

This analysis points toward the need for a socio-technical approach to AI bias that acknowledges the broader social context in which AI systems operate. As NIST researchers emphasize, "context is everything" when it comes to understanding how AI systems affect human lives [2]. AI systems do not operate in isolation but rather within complex social, cultural, and institutional environments that shape both their development and their impact.

The solution is not to abandon AI systems or to treat them as inherently problematic, but rather to develop more sophisticated approaches to human-AI collaboration that leverage the complementary strengths of humans and machines. The success of human-machine teams in contexts like Freestyle Chess and military exercises demonstrates that effective collaboration is possible when human contextual understanding is combined with machine computational power.

Moving forward, addressing AI bias will require interdisciplinary collaboration that brings together technical experts, social scientists, ethicists, and affected communities. It will require developing new frameworks for evaluating AI systems that account not just for technical performance but for social impact and equity. Most importantly, it will require maintaining human oversight and contextual understanding in AI deployment, ensuring that machines augment rather than replace human judgment in complex social contexts.

The challenges examined in this chapter are not merely technical problems to be solved but ongoing tensions that must be managed as AI systems become more deeply integrated into human society. Understanding the relationship between context and bias in AI systems is crucial for developing more responsible approaches to artificial intelligence—approaches that can harness the genuine capabilities of these systems while avoiding the systematic discrimination that emerges when machines operate without adequate contextual understanding.

The future of AI development depends on our ability to acknowledge these fundamental limitations while still pursuing the transformative potential of artificial intelligence. Only by understanding why machines cannot read context can we develop appropriate frameworks for ensuring that AI systems serve human values and promote social equity. The goal is not to create perfect AI systems but to develop approaches to human-AI collaboration that are both effective and equitable, leveraging the strengths of both humans and machines while acknowledging the limitations of each.

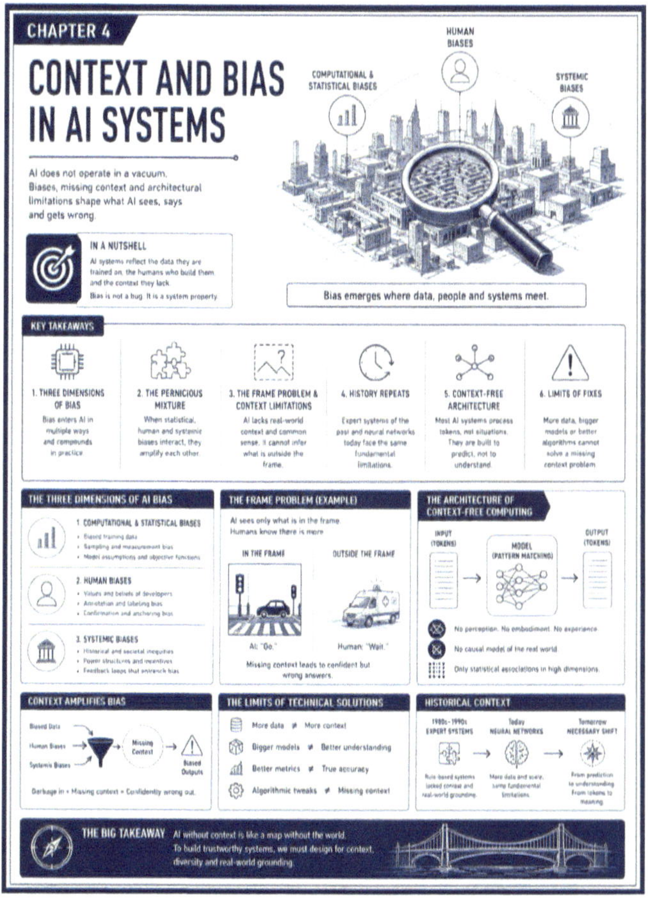
CHAPTER 4
CONTEXT AND BIAS IN AI SYSTEMS
AI does not operate in a vacuum. Biases, missing context and architectural limitations shape what AI sees, says and gets wrong.
IN A NUTSHELL
AI systems reflect the data they are trained on, the humans who build them and the context they lack.
Bias is not a bug. It is a system property.
COMPUTATIONAL & STATISTICAL BIASES
HUMAN BIASES
SYSTEMIC BIASES
Bias emerges where data, people and systems meet.
KEY TAKEAWAYS
1. THREE DIMENSIONS OF BIAS
Bias enters AI in multiple ways and compounds in practice
2. THE PERNICIOUS MIXTURE
When statistical, human and systemic biases interact, they amplify each other.
3. THE FRAME PROBLEM & CONTEXT LIMITATIONS
AI lacks real-world context and common sense. It cannot infer what is outside the frame.
4. HISTORY REPEATS
Expert systems of the past and neural networks today face the same fundamental limitations.
5. CONTEXT-FREE ARCHITECTURE
Most AI systems process tokens, not situations. They are built to predict, not to understand.
6. LIMITS OF FIXES
More data, bigger models or better algorithms cannot solve a missing context problem.
THE THREE DIMENSIONS OF AI BIAS
1. COMPUTATIONAL & STATISTICAL BIASES
Biased training data
Sampling and measurement bias
Model assumptions and objective functions
2. HUMAN BIASES
Values and beliefs of developers
Annotation and labeling bias
Confirmation and anchoring bias
3. SYSTEMIC BIASES
Historical and societal inequities
Power structures and incentives
Feedback loops that entrench bias
THE FRAME PROBLEM (EXAMPLE)
AI sees only what is in the frame.
Humans know there is more
IN THE FRAME
OUTSIDE THE FRAME
AI: "Go."
Human: "Wait."
Missing context leads to confident but wrong answers.
THE ARCHITECTURE OF CONTEXT-FREE COMPUTING
INPUT (TOKENS)
MODEL (PATTERN MATCHING)
OUTPUT (TOKENS)
No perception. No embodiment. No experience
No causal model of the real world
Only statistical associations in high dimensions
CONTEXT AMPLIFIES BIAS
Biased Data
Human Biases
Systemic Biases
Missing Context
Biased Outputs
Garbage in + Missing context = Confidently wrong out.
THE LIMITS OF TECHNICAL SOLUTIONS
More data ≠ More context
Bigger models ≠ Better understanding
Better metrics ≠ True accuracy
Algorithmic tweaks ≠ Missing context
HISTORICAL CONTEXT
1980s–1990s EXPERT SYSTEMS
Rule-based systems lacked context and real-world grounding.
Today NEURAL NETWORKS
More data and scale, same fundamental limitations.
Tomorrow NECESSARY SHIFT
From prediction to understanding. From tokens to meaning.
THE BIG TAKEAWAY
AI without context is like a map without the world.
To build trustworthy systems, we must design for context, diversity and real-world grounding.

REFERENCES

[1] Denning, P. J., & Arquilla, J. (2022, December 1). The context problem in artificial intelligence. *Communications of the ACM*, 65(12), 18-21. https://cacm.acm.org/opinion/the-context-problem-in-artificial-intelligence/

[2] Schwartz, R. (2022, March 16). There's more to AI bias than biased data, NIST report highlights. *National Institute of Standards and Technology*. https://www.nist.gov/news-events/news/2022/03/theres-more-ai-bias-biased-data-nist-report-highlights

Chapter 5: The Transformation of Human Cognition

In the span of a single generation, human beings have undergone a cognitive transformation more profound than any in recorded history. Consider the simple act of remembering a phone number: thirty years ago, most adults could recall dozens of phone numbers from memory, a cognitive skill that was essential for maintaining social connections. Today, the average smartphone user struggles to remember even their own phone number, having outsourced this basic memory function to their device. This shift represents more than mere convenience—it signals a fundamental reorganization of human cognitive architecture in response to digital technology.

The transformation extends far beyond memory to encompass the very foundations of how we think, learn, and understand the world around us. Research in neuroscience and cognitive psychology reveals that the Internet and artificial intelligence systems are producing "both acute and sustained alterations" in core areas of human cognition, changes that "may be reflected in changes in the brain" itself [1]. These alterations affect our capacity for sustained attention, our approaches to knowledge acquisition and storage, and our fundamental processes of social cognition and self-understanding.

The implications of this cognitive transformation are both profound and largely unrecognized. Unlike previous technological revolutions that primarily affected how we work or communicate, the digital revolution is reshaping the basic cognitive processes that define human consciousness. Artificial intelligence systems are not merely tools we use but cognitive partners that are actively "reshaping the cognitive and emotional landscape of human consciousness" [2]. This partnership is creating new forms of hybrid intelligence while simultaneously creating dependencies that may fundamentally alter what it means to think and know.

This chapter examines the multifaceted ways in which digital technology and artificial intelligence are transforming human cognition. We will explore how constant connectivity and information abundance are affecting our attentional capacities, how the ubiquity of external information sources is changing our memory processes and relationship to knowledge, and how digital social environments are reshaping our social cognition and sense of self. Through detailed analysis of neurological research and psychological studies, we can understand both the opportunities and risks created by this unprecedented cognitive transformation.

The central argument of this chapter is that we are witnessing the emergence of what researchers call the "online brain"—a form of human cognition that has been fundamentally altered by constant interaction with digital information systems [1]. This transformation is not simply a matter of learning new skills or adopting new tools; it represents a reorganization of cognitive architecture that affects how we process information, form memories, maintain attention, and understand ourselves in relation to others. Understanding this transformation is crucial for navigating the challenges and opportunities of an increasingly AI-augmented world.

The stakes of this cognitive transformation extend beyond individual psychology to encompass fundamental questions about human agency, creativity, and social connection. As we become increasingly dependent on artificial intelligence systems for cognitive support, we risk what psychologists describe as "cognitive constriction"—a narrowing of our mental horizons that may limit our capacity for independent thought, emotional regulation, and authentic self-discovery [2]. Yet this same transformation also offers unprecedented opportunities for cognitive enhancement and collaborative intelligence. The challenge is learning to harness these opportunities while preserving the essential qualities of human cognition that define our humanity.

The Neuroplasticity of the Digital Age

The human brain's remarkable capacity for neuroplasticity—its ability to reorganize and adapt in response to environmental demands—has enabled our species to thrive across diverse environments and master complex technologies throughout history. From the development of language to the invention of writing, major technological innovations have consistently triggered neurological adaptations that enhanced human cognitive capabilities. The digital revolution represents the latest and perhaps most dramatic chapter in this ongoing story of brain-technology co-evolution.

Research in neuroscience has convincingly demonstrated that the brain remains malleable throughout the lifespan, with various learning experiences inducing measurable changes in neuronal architecture. Second-language acquisition reshapes cortical regions associated with language processing, learning new motor skills like juggling creates structural changes in areas responsible for coordination and spatial awareness, and even formal education or exam preparation can produce detectable alterations in brain structure [1]. These findings establish that significant environmental changes can trigger corresponding neurological adaptations, setting the stage for understanding how digital technology might be reshaping human cognition.

The Smartphone as Neural Prosthetic

Perhaps the most striking example of technology-induced neuroplasticity comes from research on smartphone use and its effects on sensorimotor processing. Studies have found that even simple interactions with touchscreen interfaces produce "sustained neurocognitive alterations due to neural changes in cortical regions associated with sensory and motor processing of the hand and thumb" [1]. These changes reflect the brain's adaptation to the repetitive, precise finger movements required for touchscreen navigation—movements that were virtually unknown in human experience until the past two decades.

This finding is particularly significant because it demonstrates that neuroplastic changes can occur rapidly and in response to relatively simple technological interactions. The smartphone touchscreen represents a novel interface that requires the development of new sensorimotor skills, and the brain has adapted accordingly by reorganizing cortical representations of hand and finger movements. This adaptation suggests that more complex digital interactions—such as those involved in using artificial intelligence systems—may produce even more profound neurological changes.

The implications extend beyond mere motor adaptation to encompass fundamental changes in how we interact with information and make decisions. The smartphone has become what researchers describe as a "neural prosthetic"—an external device that extends and augments human cognitive capabilities while simultaneously creating dependencies that alter how we think and remember. When we reflexively reach for our phones to answer questions, navigate unfamiliar locations, or capture memories through photographs, we are engaging in a form of cognitive offloading that may be reshaping the neural pathways associated with memory, attention, and problem-solving.

Cognitive Reserve and Digital Engagement

The concept of cognitive reserve—the brain's ability to withstand insult from age and pathology—provides crucial insights into how digital technology might affect long-term cognitive health. Research has shown that individuals who maintain cognitively engaging lifestyles throughout their lives tend to preserve cognitive function better as they age, while those who adopt "less engaging lifestyles" may experience accelerated cognitive decline [1]. This finding raises important questions about whether digital technology enhances or diminishes cognitive engagement.

On one hand, digital technology offers unprecedented opportunities for cognitive stimulation and learning. The Internet provides access to vast repositories of information, online courses enable lifelong learning, and digital games can challenge various cognitive skills. For older adults in particular, digital engagement may offer new pathways for maintaining cognitive reserve and preventing age-related decline. Research suggests that "digital natives could feasibly develop forms of 'online cognition' in the aging brain, whereby older adults can increasingly take advantage of digital technologies to support cognitive function" [1].

However, the quality and nature of digital engagement appears to be crucial. Not all digital activities provide the same cognitive benefits, and some forms of technology use may actually be detrimental to cognitive health. A randomized controlled trial found that six weeks of engaging in an online role-playing game caused "significant reductions in grey matter within the orbitofrontal cortex—a brain region implicated in impulse control and decision making" [1]. This finding suggests that certain types of digital engagement, particularly those that involve immersive virtual environments, may have negative effects on brain structure and function.

The Paradox of Digital Cognitive Enhancement

The neuroplastic effects of digital technology create a fundamental paradox: the same technologies that offer unprecedented opportunities for cognitive enhancement may also create dependencies that diminish certain cognitive capabilities. This paradox is particularly evident in the realm of memory and information processing, where digital tools can both augment and replace human cognitive functions.

Consider how GPS navigation systems have affected spatial cognition. While these systems enable us to navigate complex urban environments with ease, research suggests that heavy reliance on GPS may be associated with reduced activity in the hippocampus—a brain region crucial for spatial memory and navigation [1]. Similarly, the constant availability of search engines may be reducing our motivation to encode information in long-term memory, leading to what researchers call the "Google effect" or "digital amnesia."

This paradox reflects a broader tension in human-technology relationships: technologies that make cognitive tasks easier may simultaneously reduce our capacity to perform those tasks independently. The brain's plasticity means that it adapts to the cognitive demands of the environment, and if digital tools consistently reduce those demands, the brain may reorganize accordingly. This can lead to a form of cognitive atrophy where skills that are not regularly exercised begin to deteriorate.

Developmental Implications for Digital Natives

The neuroplastic effects of digital technology are particularly significant for children and adolescents, whose brains are still developing and are therefore more susceptible to environmental influences. Many cognitive processes, particularly those related to executive function and social cognition, "are not entirely innate, but rather are strongly influenced by environmental factors" [1]. This means that the digital environment in which young people are developing may have profound and lasting effects on their cognitive architecture.

Research has identified several areas of particular concern for digital natives—individuals who have grown up immersed in digital technology from an early age. These include potential effects on attention span and the ability to engage in sustained, focused thinking; changes in memory processes and the relationship to knowledge; and alterations in social cognition and emotional regulation. While some of these changes may represent adaptive responses to a digital environment, others may create challenges for functioning in non-digital contexts.

The developing brain's plasticity means that early exposure to digital technology may create cognitive patterns that persist throughout life. If children learn to rely heavily on external digital systems for memory, attention regulation, and problem-solving, these dependencies may become deeply ingrained in their cognitive architecture. This raises important questions about how to balance the benefits of digital technology with the need to develop robust, independent cognitive capabilities.

Implications for Cognitive Development

Understanding the neuroplastic effects of digital technology is crucial for making informed decisions about how to integrate these tools into human life and society. The brain's adaptability means that we have some degree of choice in how digital technology shapes our cognition, but this choice requires awareness of the mechanisms involved and intentional effort to guide the process.

The research suggests that the key factor is not whether we use digital technology, but how we use it. Technologies that challenge and engage cognitive processes may enhance brain function, while those that replace or bypass cognitive processes may lead to atrophy. This distinction has important implications for education, workplace design, and personal technology use.

Moving forward, the challenge will be learning to harness the cognitive enhancement potential of digital technology while avoiding the pitfalls of cognitive dependency and atrophy. This requires developing new forms of digital literacy that go beyond technical skills to encompass understanding of how technology affects cognition and brain function. Only by understanding the neuroplastic effects of digital technology can we hope to shape its development and use in ways that enhance rather than diminish human cognitive capabilities.

The Three Domains of Cognitive Transformation

The transformation of human cognition in the digital age manifests across three interconnected domains that collectively define how we think, learn, and interact with the world. Research in cognitive psychology and neuroscience has identified attention, memory, and social cognition as the primary areas where digital technology is producing measurable changes in human cognitive processes [1].

Understanding these transformations is crucial for grasping the full scope of how artificial intelligence and digital systems are reshaping human consciousness.

Attention: The Fragmentation of Focus

The most immediately apparent effect of digital technology on human cognition involves our capacity for sustained attention. The "constantly evolving stream of online information encourages our divided attention across multiple media sources, at the expense of sustained concentration" [1]. This shift from sustained to divided attention represents a fundamental change in how humans process information and engage with cognitive tasks.

Traditional models of human attention were built around the assumption that focused, sustained attention was the optimal state for learning, problem-solving, and creative work. The ability to maintain concentration on a single task for extended periods was considered a hallmark of cognitive maturity and intellectual achievement. However, the digital environment rewards and reinforces very different attentional patterns, favoring rapid switching between multiple information streams over deep engagement with any single source.

The constant influx of notifications, alerts, and updates creates what researchers describe as an "attention economy" where digital platforms compete for user engagement through increasingly sophisticated methods of capturing and maintaining attention. These systems are designed to interrupt whatever users are doing and redirect their focus to new content, creating a cognitive environment characterized by frequent task-switching and divided attention.

Neurological research reveals that this shift in attentional patterns is producing measurable changes in brain structure and function. Studies using neuroimaging techniques have found differences in the prefrontal cortex—the brain region responsible for executive attention and cognitive control—between heavy internet users and those with more limited digital exposure. These changes appear to affect the ability to filter irrelevant information and maintain focus on goal-directed activities.

The implications of attentional fragmentation extend beyond individual cognitive performance to encompass broader questions about learning, creativity, and intellectual development. Deep learning and creative insight often require sustained periods of focused attention that allow for the development of complex ideas and the formation of novel connections between concepts. If digital technology is systematically undermining our capacity for sustained attention, it may be limiting our ability to engage in the kinds of deep thinking that drive innovation and understanding.

However, the picture is not entirely negative. Some research suggests that experience with digital multitasking may enhance certain cognitive skills, particularly those related to task-switching and parallel processing. Individuals who have grown up in digital environments may develop enhanced abilities to rapidly assess and prioritize multiple information streams, skills that are increasingly valuable in complex, information-rich environments.

Memory: The Externalization of Knowledge

Perhaps no aspect of human cognition has been more profoundly affected by digital technology than memory. The ubiquity of external information sources is fundamentally changing "the way we retrieve, store, and even value knowledge" [1]. This transformation represents a shift from internal to external memory storage that may be as significant as the invention of writing itself.

The phenomenon known as the "Google effect" or "digital amnesia" illustrates how the availability of external information sources affects human memory processes. When people know that information will be readily available through digital search, they are less likely to encode that information in long-term memory. Instead, they tend to remember where to find information rather than the information itself. This represents a form of cognitive offloading where external systems take over functions previously performed by human memory.

This shift has profound implications for how we understand knowledge and expertise. Traditional models of expertise emphasized the importance of having extensive factual knowledge readily available in memory, allowing experts to make rapid connections and generate insights based on their accumulated knowledge. However, in a world where factual information is instantly accessible through digital search, the value of memorized knowledge may be diminishing relative to skills like information evaluation, synthesis, and creative application.

The externalization of memory also affects how we form and maintain personal identity. Autobiographical memory—our recollection of personal experiences and life events—plays a crucial role in maintaining a coherent sense of self over time. However, the increasing tendency to document life experiences through digital photography and social media may be affecting how we encode and recall personal memories. Some research suggests that the act of photographing experiences may actually reduce our ability to remember them, as the external recording device takes over the memory function.

The implications extend to educational and professional contexts where the balance between memorized knowledge and external information access is being renegotiated. Educational systems that were designed around the assumption that students needed to memorize large amounts of factual information are being challenged to adapt to a world where such information is instantly accessible. This shift requires new approaches to learning that emphasize critical thinking, information evaluation, and creative synthesis over rote memorization.

Social Cognition: The Digital Self

The third domain of cognitive transformation involves social cognition—how we understand ourselves and others in social contexts. Digital technology has created new forms of social interaction that "resemble and evoke real-world social processes" while simultaneously creating "a new interplay between the Internet and our social lives, including our self-concepts and self-esteem" [1].

Social media platforms and digital communication tools have fundamentally altered how we form and maintain relationships, present ourselves to others, and understand our place in social hierarchies. These platforms create what researchers describe as "curated selves"—carefully constructed digital personas that may differ significantly from our offline identities. The process of creating and maintaining these digital selves requires new forms of social cognition that were unknown in pre-digital environments.

The quantification of social interaction through likes, shares, comments, and follower counts has created new metrics for social validation and self-worth. These metrics provide immediate feedback on social performance in ways that can be both rewarding and anxiety-provoking. Research suggests that heavy social media use is associated with increased rates of anxiety and depression, particularly among young people who are still developing their sense of identity and self-worth.

The digital environment also affects how we process social information and make judgments about others. Online interactions often lack the rich contextual cues available in face-to-face communication, requiring us to make social judgments based on limited information. This can lead to misunderstandings and conflicts, but it may also be developing new skills for interpreting digital communication cues and managing online relationships.

The phenomenon of "context collapse" in digital environments—where different social contexts and audiences are merged into a single platform—creates new challenges for social cognition. In offline environments, we naturally adjust our behavior and self-presentation based on social context, but digital platforms often require us to present a single, unified identity to diverse audiences. This can create cognitive strain and may be affecting how we understand and manage our multiple social roles and identities.

The Interconnected Nature of Cognitive Change

These three domains of cognitive transformation—attention, memory, and social cognition—do not operate independently but rather interact in complex ways that amplify and modify each other's effects. Changes in attentional patterns affect how we encode memories and process social information. The externalization of memory changes how we allocate attention and affects our social interactions. Digital social environments shape both our attentional patterns and our memory processes.

Understanding these interconnections is crucial for grasping the full scope of cognitive transformation in the digital age. The changes occurring in human cognition are not simply additive but represent a systemic reorganization of cognitive architecture that affects how we think, learn, and relate to others. This reorganization creates both opportunities and challenges that require careful consideration as we navigate an increasingly digital world.

The research suggests that we are in the early stages of a cognitive transformation that may be as significant as any in human history. The challenge is learning to guide this transformation in ways that enhance rather than diminish human cognitive capabilities while preserving the essential qualities that define human consciousness and creativity.

In Conclusion

The transformation of human cognition in the digital age represents one of the most significant developments in the history of human consciousness. As we have seen throughout this chapter, the integration of digital technology and artificial intelligence into daily life is producing measurable changes in brain structure and function that affect how we think, remember, and relate to others. These changes are not merely superficial adaptations to new tools but represent a fundamental reorganization of cognitive architecture that may define human consciousness for generations to come.

The neuroplastic nature of the human brain means that we are active participants in this transformation rather than passive recipients of technological change. The brain's remarkable capacity to adapt to environmental demands has enabled our species to thrive across diverse contexts throughout history, and it is now enabling us to adapt to the unprecedented cognitive demands of the digital age. However, this adaptability also means that we bear responsibility for guiding the direction of cognitive change through our choices about how we design, deploy, and use digital technologies.

The three domains of cognitive transformation—attention, memory, and social cognition—reveal both the opportunities and challenges created by digital technology. The fragmentation of attention may be undermining our capacity for deep, sustained thinking, but it may also be developing new skills for managing complex, information-rich environments. The externalization of memory may be reducing our reliance on internal knowledge storage, but it may also be freeing cognitive resources for higher-order thinking and creative synthesis. The digitization of social interaction may be creating new forms of anxiety and identity confusion, but it may also be expanding our capacity for connection and collaboration across traditional boundaries.

Understanding these transformations is crucial for making informed decisions about the future of human-AI collaboration. The research suggests that the key factor is not whether we use digital technology, but how we use it. Technologies that challenge and engage cognitive processes may enhance brain function and cognitive capabilities, while those that replace or bypass cognitive processes may lead to atrophy and dependency. This distinction has profound implications for education, workplace design, and personal technology use.

The emergence of the "online brain" represents both an opportunity and a warning. On one hand, the integration of human and artificial intelligence offers unprecedented possibilities for cognitive enhancement and collaborative problem-solving. The combination of human creativity, contextual understanding, and emotional intelligence with artificial systems' computational power and information processing capabilities could enable new forms of hybrid intelligence that surpass the capabilities of either humans or machines alone.

On the other hand, the risk of cognitive constriction and dependency is real and significant. If we become overly reliant on external systems for basic cognitive functions, we may lose essential capabilities that define human consciousness and agency. The challenge is learning to harness the benefits of cognitive offloading while maintaining the cognitive independence and flexibility that enable creativity, critical thinking, and authentic self-expression.

The implications extend beyond individual psychology to encompass fundamental questions about human society and culture. If digital technology is systematically altering how we think and remember, it is also changing how we create and transmit knowledge, how we form and maintain relationships, and how we understand ourselves and our place in the world. These changes may be creating new forms of human capability and connection, but they may also be undermining traditional sources of meaning and identity.

Moving forward, the challenge will be developing new forms of digital wisdom that enable us to navigate the cognitive transformation of the digital age with intention and awareness. This requires understanding not just how to use digital tools effectively, but how those tools are changing us and what we want to preserve or enhance about human cognition and consciousness.

The transformation of human cognition is not a distant future possibility but a present reality that is unfolding around us every day. Every time we reach for our smartphones to answer a question, rely on GPS to navigate, or engage with AI systems for cognitive support, we are participating in this transformation. The question is not whether this transformation will continue—it almost certainly will—but whether we can guide it in directions that enhance rather than diminish human flourishing.

The research examined in this chapter suggests that we have more agency in this process than we might assume. The brain's plasticity means that cognitive change is not predetermined but rather emerges from the interaction between our neural architecture and our environmental choices. By making conscious decisions about how we design and use digital technologies, we can influence the direction of cognitive transformation and work toward outcomes that preserve the best of human cognition while embracing the possibilities of human-AI collaboration.

The future of human cognition will be shaped by the choices we make today about how to integrate artificial intelligence into human life and society. Understanding the mechanisms of cognitive transformation is the first step toward making those choices wisely and ensuring that the digital revolution enhances rather than diminishes the remarkable cognitive capabilities that define our humanity.

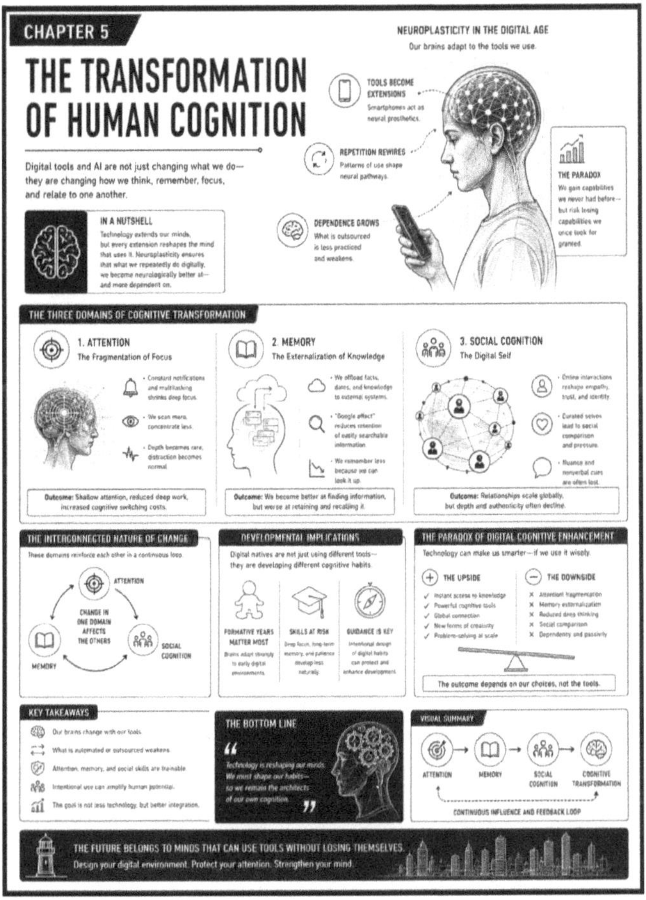

CHAPTER 5
THE TRANSFORMATION OF HUMAN COGNITION
Digital tools and AI are not just changing what we do—they are changing how we think, remember, focus, and relate to one another.
IN A NUTSHELL
Technology extends our minds, but every extension reshapes the mind that uses it. Neuroplasticity ensures that what we repeatedly do digitally, we become neurologically better at—and more dependent on.
NEUROPLASTICITY IN THE DIGITAL AGE
Our brains adapt to the tools we use.
TOOLS BECOME EXTENSIONS
Smartphones act as neural prosthetics.
REPETITION REWIRES
Patterns of use shape neural pathways.
DEPENDENCE GROWS
What is outsourced is less practiced and weakens.
THE PARADOX
We gain capabilities we never had before—but risk losing capabilities we once took for granted.
THE THREE DOMAINS OF COGNITIVE TRANSFORMATION
1. ATTENTION
The Fragmentation of Focus
Constant notifications and multitasking shrinks deep focus.
We scan more, concentrate less.
Depth becomes rare, distraction becomes normal.
Outcome: Shallow attention, reduced deep work, increased cognitive switching costs.
2. MEMORY
The Externalization of Knowledge
We offload facts, dates, and knowledge to external systems.
"Google effect" reduces retention of easily searchable information.
We remember less because we can look it up.
Outcome: We become better at finding information, but worse at retaining and recalling it.
3. SOCIAL COGNITION
The Digital Self
Online interactions reshape empathy, trust, and identity.
Curated selves lead to social comparison and pressure.
Nuance and nonverbal cues are often lost.
Outcome: Relationships scale globally, but depth and authenticity often decline.
THE INTERCONNECTED NATURE OF CHANGE
These domains reinforce each other in a continuous loop.
ATTENTION
CHANGE IN ONE DOMAIN AFFECTS THE OTHERS
MEMORY
SOCIAL COGNITION
DEVELOPMENTAL IMPLICATIONS
Digital natives are not just using different tools—they are developing different cognitive habits.
FORMATIVE YEARS MATTER MOST
Brains adapt strongly to early digital environments.
SKILLS AT RISK
Deep focus, long-term memory, and patience develop less naturally.
GUIDANCE IS KEY
Intentional design of digital habits can protect and enhance development.
THE PARADOX OF DIGITAL COGNITIVE ENHANCEMENT
Technology can make us smarter—if we use it wisely.
THE UPSIDE
✓ Instant access to knowledge
✓ Powerful cognitive tools
✓ Global connection
✓ New forms of creativity
✓ Problem-solving at scale
THE DOWNSIDE
✗ Attention fragmentation
✗ Memory externalization
✗ Reduced deep thinking
✗ Social comparison
✗ Dependency and passivity
The outcome depends on our choices, not the tools.
KEY TAKEAWAYS
Our brains change with our tools.
What is automated or outsourced weakens.
Attention, memory, and social skills are trainable.
Intentional use can amplify human potential.
The goal is not less technology, but better integration.
THE BOTTOM LINE
"Technology is reshaping our minds. We must shape our habits—so we remain the architects of our own cognition."
VISUAL SUMMARY
ATTENTION
MEMORY
SOCIAL COGNITION
COGNITIVE TRANSFORMATION
CONTINUOUS INFLUENCE AND FEEDBACK LOOP
THE FUTURE BELONGS TO MINDS THAT CAN USE TOOLS WITHOUT LOSING THEMSELVES.
Design your digital environment. Protect your attention. Strengthen your mind.

REFERENCES

[1] Firth, J., Torous, J., Stubbs, B., Firth, J. A., Steiner, G. Z., Smith, L., Alvarez-Jimenez, M., Gleeson, J., Vancampfort, D., Armitage, C. J., & Sarris, J. (2019). The "online brain": how the Internet may be changing our cognition. *World Psychiatry*, 18(2), 119-129. https://pmc.ncbi.nlm.nih.gov/articles/PMC6502424/

[2] Walther, C. C. (2025, June 3). The psychology of AI's impact on human cognition. *Psychology Today*. https://www.psychologytoday.com/us/blog/harnessing-hybrid-intelligence/202506/the-psychology-of-ais-impact-on-human-cognition

Chapter 6: The Future of Thinking

As we stand at the threshold of an unprecedented era in human history, the very nature of thinking itself is being redefined. The convergence of artificial intelligence, cognitive enhancement technologies, and our deepening understanding of neuroplasticity is creating possibilities for human cognition that were unimaginable just decades ago. We are witnessing the emergence of what researchers call "hybrid intelligence"—a new form of cognitive capability that combines "the computational strengths of artificial intelligence with the holistic comprehension of natural intelligence, leading to more sustainable, creative, and trustworthy results" [1].

This transformation extends far beyond the simple adoption of new tools or technologies. We are entering an age where the boundaries between human and artificial intelligence are becoming increasingly fluid, where cognitive enhancement is moving from science fiction to scientific reality, and where the fundamental questions about what it means to think, know, and understand are being rewritten. The implications of this cognitive revolution will shape not only how we work and learn but how we define human consciousness and agency in an increasingly AI-augmented world.

The future of thinking is not predetermined but rather emerges from the choices we make today about how to design, deploy, and integrate cognitive technologies into human life and society. As one researcher notes, "implementing hybrid intelligence is not simply a technology upgrade but a cultural transformation" [1]. This transformation requires us to navigate complex questions about cognitive enhancement, human-AI collaboration, and the preservation of essential human capabilities while embracing the unprecedented opportunities for cognitive augmentation.

This chapter explores the emerging landscape of human cognition in an AI-augmented future. We will examine the concept of hybrid intelligence and its potential to create new forms of cognitive capability that surpass what either humans or machines can achieve alone. We will investigate the rapidly advancing field of cognitive enhancement, from biochemical interventions to behavioral strategies that promise to augment human mental capabilities. We will also consider the challenges and opportunities created by this cognitive transformation, including questions about equity, authenticity, and the preservation of human agency.

The central argument of this chapter is that we are witnessing the emergence of a new cognitive paradigm—one that transcends the traditional boundaries between human and artificial intelligence to create hybrid forms of thinking that could fundamentally enhance human capability and understanding. However, realizing this potential requires careful attention to the design and implementation of cognitive technologies, ensuring that they enhance rather than replace essential human capabilities and that their benefits are distributed equitably across society.

The stakes of this transformation are enormous. The choices we make about cognitive enhancement and human-AI collaboration will determine whether the future of thinking enhances human flourishing or creates new forms of dependency and inequality. Understanding the possibilities and pitfalls of this cognitive revolution is essential for navigating toward a future where technology amplifies the best of human intelligence while preserving the qualities that make us uniquely human.

Hybrid Intelligence: The Convergence of Human and Artificial Cognition

The concept of hybrid intelligence represents a fundamental shift in how we think about the relationship between human and artificial intelligence. Rather than viewing AI as a replacement for human cognition or as a separate, competing form of intelligence, hybrid intelligence envisions a collaborative model where human and artificial capabilities are integrated to create cognitive systems that exceed the capabilities of either component alone. This approach recognizes that human and artificial intelligence have complementary strengths and limitations, and that their combination can produce more robust, creative, and trustworthy outcomes than either could achieve independently.

The Complementary Nature of Human and Artificial Intelligence

The foundation of hybrid intelligence lies in understanding the fundamental differences between human and artificial cognition. Artificial intelligence systems excel at processing vast amounts of data, identifying patterns across large datasets, performing rapid calculations, and maintaining consistent performance without fatigue. They can analyze thousands of similar cases in seconds, process multiple information streams simultaneously, and provide data-driven insights based on comprehensive analysis of available information.

Human intelligence, by contrast, brings qualities that remain beyond the reach of current AI systems: contextual understanding, emotional intelligence, creative insight, ethical reasoning, and the ability to navigate ambiguous or novel situations. Humans excel at understanding the broader implications of decisions, considering multiple stakeholder perspectives, and making judgments that incorporate values and meaning alongside data and logic. As researchers note, "natural intelligence offers a holistic understanding of human complexity and the consequences of AI on society" [1].

This complementarity is perhaps best illustrated through real-world examples of successful human-AI collaboration. Consider the case of a neurosurgeon facing a complex, high-risk brain surgery. Despite years of experience, the case presents unpredictable variables that challenge even expert judgment. Rather than relying solely on experience, the surgeon uses an AI-powered surgical planning system that analyzes thousands of similar cases in seconds, providing data-driven insights about optimal approaches and potential complications.

The AI system extends the surgeon's capabilities by processing far more information than any human could analyze, identifying patterns across vast datasets, and providing real-time monitoring during the procedure. However, the human surgeon brings irreplaceable qualities: the ability to adapt to unexpected situations, make ethical judgments about risk and benefit, communicate with the patient and family, and integrate technical considerations with broader human values. The AI continues monitoring during surgery, flagging anomalies and suggesting adjustments, while the surgeon makes final decisions based on the combination of AI analysis and human judgment.

This example illustrates the key principle of hybrid intelligence: neither the AI nor the human could achieve optimal outcomes alone. The AI lacks the contextual understanding, ethical reasoning, and adaptive capabilities of the human surgeon. The human surgeon, despite extensive training and experience, cannot match the AI's ability to process vast amounts of data and identify subtle patterns across thousands of cases. Together, they create a cognitive system that is more capable, reliable, and effective than either could be independently.

Organizational Implementation of Hybrid Intelligence

The successful implementation of hybrid intelligence requires more than simply adding AI tools to existing human workflows. It demands a fundamental rethinking of how cognitive work is organized, how decisions are made, and how human and artificial capabilities are integrated. Research suggests that "organizations can curate hybrid intelligence by investing in algorithmic fluency and humanistic insights" [1].

Algorithmic fluency involves developing understanding of how AI systems work, what their capabilities and limitations are, and how to effectively collaborate with them. This goes beyond basic technical skills to encompass understanding of AI decision-making processes, awareness of potential biases and errors, and knowledge of how to interpret and validate AI outputs. Workers need to understand not just how to use AI tools but how to think with them—how to frame problems in ways that leverage AI capabilities while maintaining human oversight and judgment.

Humanistic insights, meanwhile, involve preserving and developing the distinctly human capabilities that complement AI systems. This includes emotional intelligence, ethical reasoning, creative thinking, and the ability to understand and navigate complex social and cultural contexts. Organizations implementing hybrid intelligence must ensure that human workers continue to develop these capabilities rather than allowing them to atrophy through over-reliance on AI systems.

The cultural transformation required for hybrid intelligence implementation involves several key elements. First, organizations must move beyond viewing AI as a tool for automation toward seeing it as a partner in cognitive work. This requires developing new models of human-AI collaboration that preserve human agency while leveraging AI capabilities. Second, organizations must invest in training and development that prepares workers for hybrid intelligence environments, focusing on both technical skills and the human capabilities that complement AI systems.

Third, organizations must develop new approaches to decision-making that effectively integrate human and artificial intelligence. This involves creating processes that leverage AI analysis while preserving human judgment, establishing clear roles and responsibilities for human and AI components, and developing mechanisms for resolving conflicts between human and AI recommendations.

The Promise of Augmented Creativity and Innovation

One of the most exciting possibilities of hybrid intelligence lies in its potential to augment human creativity and innovation. Traditional models of creativity emphasize the importance of human intuition, imagination, and the ability to make novel connections between disparate concepts. While these capabilities remain uniquely human, AI systems can enhance creative processes by providing new sources of inspiration, identifying unexpected patterns and connections, and enabling rapid exploration of creative possibilities.

In fields ranging from scientific research to artistic creation, hybrid intelligence is already demonstrating its potential to enhance human creativity. AI systems can analyze vast databases of scientific literature to identify potential research directions, generate multiple design variations for creative projects, or provide real-time feedback on creative works in progress. However, the creative vision, aesthetic judgment, and meaningful interpretation remain distinctly human contributions.

The key to successful creative collaboration between humans and AI lies in understanding how to structure the interaction to leverage the strengths of both. AI systems excel at generating variations, identifying patterns, and processing large amounts of information, while humans excel at evaluating meaning, making aesthetic judgments, and understanding cultural and emotional contexts. When these capabilities are effectively combined, they can produce creative outcomes that neither humans nor AI could achieve alone.

Challenges and Considerations for Hybrid Intelligence

Despite its promise, the development of hybrid intelligence faces several significant challenges that must be addressed to realize its full potential. One of the primary challenges involves maintaining appropriate human agency and oversight in hybrid systems. As AI capabilities continue to advance, there is a risk that human workers may become overly dependent on AI recommendations, leading to a degradation of human judgment and decision-making capabilities.

Another challenge involves ensuring that hybrid intelligence systems are designed to enhance rather than replace human capabilities. The goal should be to create systems that make humans more capable and effective rather than systems that make humans redundant. This requires careful attention to the design of human-AI interfaces and workflows, ensuring that humans remain actively engaged in cognitive processes rather than becoming passive recipients of AI outputs.

Equity and access represent additional challenges for hybrid intelligence implementation. If hybrid intelligence systems provide significant cognitive advantages, ensuring equitable access to these systems becomes crucial for preventing the emergence of new forms of inequality. Organizations and societies must consider how to make hybrid intelligence capabilities available broadly rather than concentrating them among privileged groups.

The development of hybrid intelligence also raises important questions about accountability and responsibility. When decisions are made through human-AI collaboration, determining responsibility for outcomes becomes more complex. Clear frameworks for accountability must be developed that appropriately distribute responsibility between human and AI components while ensuring that human oversight and judgment remain central to important decisions.

The Future Trajectory of Human-AI Collaboration

Looking toward the future, the trajectory of hybrid intelligence development will likely be shaped by several key trends. First, AI systems will become increasingly sophisticated in their ability to understand and respond to human cognitive patterns, enabling more natural and effective collaboration. Second, human workers will develop greater fluency in working with AI systems, leading to more effective hybrid cognitive processes.

Third, new forms of human-AI interface will emerge that enable more seamless integration of human and artificial intelligence. These may include brain-computer interfaces, augmented reality systems, and other technologies that reduce the cognitive overhead of human-AI collaboration. Fourth, organizational structures and processes will evolve to better support hybrid intelligence, with new roles, workflows, and decision-making processes designed specifically for human-AI collaboration.

The ultimate goal of hybrid intelligence is not to replace human thinking but to augment it—to create cognitive systems that preserve and enhance the best of human intelligence while leveraging the computational power and analytical capabilities of AI systems. Success in this endeavor will require ongoing attention to the design and implementation of hybrid systems, ensuring that they enhance human capability and agency rather than diminishing them.

As we move toward this hybrid future, the challenge will be maintaining the delicate balance between leveraging AI capabilities and preserving essential human qualities. The future of thinking will be shaped by our ability to create hybrid intelligence systems that are not only more capable than their individual components but also more aligned with human values and more supportive of human flourishing.

The Cognitive Enhancement Revolution: Hacking the Brain

Parallel to the development of hybrid intelligence, we are witnessing an unprecedented expansion in technologies and strategies designed to enhance human cognitive capabilities directly. This "cognitive enhancement revolution" represents a fundamental shift from external tools that support thinking to interventions that modify the brain's own functioning. As researchers note, "just like the hacking culture in the realm of computer software and hardware, an increasing number of individuals experiment with strategies to creatively overcome the natural limitations of human cognitive capacity—in other words, to hack brain function" [2].

The present era is unique because "not only the challenges are growing rapidly but so are technologies that promise to meet them" [2]. The increasing complexity of modern life, with its demands for rapid information processing, sustained attention, and continuous learning, has created unprecedented pressure on human cognitive systems. Simultaneously, advances in neuroscience, pharmacology, and technology have opened new possibilities for enhancing cognitive function that were previously confined to science fiction.

The Multidimensional Nature of Cognitive Enhancement

Cognitive enhancement is far from a monolithic phenomenon. Research reveals that "there is not one cognitive enhancer that augments brain function per se, but a great variety of interventions that can be clustered into biochemical, physical, and behavioral enhancement strategies" [2]. Understanding these different approaches and their implications is crucial for navigating the future of cognitive enhancement.

The scientific framework for understanding cognitive enhancement involves seven essential dimensions that determine how different interventions work and what their implications might be. These dimensions include the mode of action (how the enhancement works), the cognitive domain targeted (which mental functions are affected), personal factors (how individual differences influence effectiveness), time scale (immediate versus long-term effects), side effects (risks and unintended consequences), availability (accessibility and cost), and social acceptance (ethical and cultural considerations) [2].

This multidimensional framework reveals that cognitive enhancement interventions differ dramatically in their mechanisms, effects, and implications. A pharmaceutical intervention that enhances working memory through neurotransmitter modulation operates very differently from a behavioral intervention that improves attention through meditation training. Understanding these differences is essential for making informed decisions about cognitive enhancement and for developing appropriate regulatory and ethical frameworks.

Biochemical Strategies: From Coffee to Smart Drugs

Biochemical approaches to cognitive enhancement represent perhaps the most familiar and widely used category of interventions. These range from everyday substances like caffeine and glucose to sophisticated pharmaceutical compounds designed specifically for cognitive enhancement. The long history of biochemical cognitive enhancement demonstrates that humans have always sought to modify their mental states through chemical means.

The most widely used biochemical cognitive enhancers are substances that most people consume regularly without thinking of them as enhancement technologies. Caffeine, found in coffee, tea, and energy drinks, has "demonstrated cognition-enhancing effects in numerous studies" [2]. Glucose, the brain's primary fuel source, can enhance memory processes and neural activation in memory-related brain regions. These substances work by modifying neurotransmitter systems and energy metabolism in ways that improve cognitive performance.

Beyond these common substances, research has identified numerous other biochemical interventions with cognitive enhancement potential. Nutritional components such as flavonoids found in cocoa, curcumin from curry powder, omega-3 fatty acids, and various vitamins and minerals have shown evidence of cognitive benefits. Traditional herbal remedies, including salvia and various Asian medicinal plants like Bacopa monnieri, have been studied for their potential cognitive effects.

More controversial are pharmaceutical interventions designed specifically for cognitive enhancement. These "smart drugs" or nootropics include medications originally developed for treating cognitive disorders but used by healthy individuals to enhance performance. Examples include stimulants like modafinil and amphetamines, which can improve alertness and focus, and cholinesterase inhibitors originally developed for Alzheimer's disease, which may enhance memory function in healthy individuals.

The appeal of biochemical cognitive enhancement lies in its relative simplicity and immediate effects. Taking a pill or consuming a beverage requires minimal effort and can produce noticeable improvements in cognitive performance within hours. However, biochemical interventions also raise significant concerns about safety, long-term effects, and the potential for dependency or abuse.

Physical Interventions: Stimulating the Brain

Physical approaches to cognitive enhancement involve direct manipulation of brain activity through various forms of stimulation or modification of physiological states. These interventions work by altering neural activity patterns, improving brain connectivity, or optimizing the physiological conditions that support cognitive function.

Brain stimulation techniques represent one of the most promising areas of physical cognitive enhancement. Transcranial direct current stimulation (tDCS) and transcranial magnetic stimulation (TMS) can temporarily enhance cognitive performance by modifying neural activity in specific brain regions. These techniques can improve working memory, attention, learning, and other cognitive functions by increasing or decreasing neural activity in targeted areas.

More invasive approaches include deep brain stimulation (DBS) and other neurosurgical interventions that can produce dramatic improvements in cognitive function. While these techniques are currently used primarily for treating neurological and psychiatric disorders, they raise the possibility of more direct forms of cognitive enhancement in the future.

Physical exercise represents another important category of physical cognitive enhancement. Regular aerobic exercise has been shown to improve cognitive function across multiple domains, including memory, attention, and executive function. Exercise works by promoting neuroplasticity, increasing blood flow to the brain, and stimulating the production of neurotrophic factors that support brain health.

Sleep optimization is another crucial physical intervention for cognitive enhancement. Quality sleep is essential for memory consolidation, attention regulation, and overall cognitive performance. Interventions that improve sleep quality or optimize sleep timing can produce significant improvements in cognitive function.

Behavioral Strategies: Training the Mind

Behavioral approaches to cognitive enhancement focus on training and practice to improve cognitive capabilities. These interventions work by leveraging the brain's plasticity to strengthen neural networks and develop more efficient cognitive processes. Unlike biochemical or physical interventions, behavioral strategies typically require sustained effort and practice but can produce lasting improvements in cognitive function.

Cognitive training programs represent one of the most extensively studied behavioral approaches to enhancement. These programs involve repeated practice on tasks designed to improve specific cognitive abilities such as working memory, attention, or processing speed. While the effectiveness of cognitive training has been debated, research suggests that well-designed programs can produce improvements that transfer to real-world cognitive tasks.

Meditation and mindfulness practices represent another important category of behavioral cognitive enhancement. Regular meditation practice has been shown to improve attention regulation, emotional control, and various aspects of cognitive function. These practices work by training the brain's attention networks and promoting changes in brain structure and function that support improved cognitive performance.

Educational interventions and learning strategies also function as forms of cognitive enhancement. Techniques such as spaced repetition, elaborative encoding, and metacognitive training can significantly improve learning and memory performance. These approaches work by optimizing how information is encoded, stored, and retrieved in memory systems.

The Promise and Perils of Cognitive Enhancement

The rapid advancement of cognitive enhancement technologies offers unprecedented opportunities for improving human cognitive capabilities. These interventions could help address the growing cognitive demands of modern life, support healthy aging, and enable individuals to reach their full cognitive potential. For students, workers, and professionals facing increasing cognitive demands, enhancement technologies could provide crucial support for performance and well-being.

However, cognitive enhancement also raises significant ethical, social, and practical concerns that must be carefully considered. Questions of safety and long-term effects are paramount, particularly for biochemical and physical interventions that directly modify brain function. Many enhancement technologies have not been extensively studied for long-term use in healthy populations, and their safety profiles remain uncertain.

Equity and access represent another major concern. If cognitive enhancement technologies provide significant advantages, ensuring equitable access becomes crucial for preventing the emergence of new forms of inequality. The possibility of "cognitive divides" between enhanced and unenhanced individuals could exacerbate existing social inequalities and create new forms of discrimination.

Authenticity and identity concerns arise when considering how cognitive enhancement might affect personal identity and achievement. If cognitive capabilities are significantly modified through external interventions, questions arise about whether achievements represent genuine personal accomplishment or the effects of enhancement technologies. These concerns are particularly relevant in competitive contexts such as education and employment.

Regulatory and Ethical Frameworks

The development of cognitive enhancement technologies requires careful consideration of regulatory and ethical frameworks that can guide their development and use. Current regulatory systems, designed primarily for treating medical conditions, may be inadequate for addressing the unique challenges posed by enhancement technologies used by healthy individuals.

Key principles for cognitive enhancement governance include safety and efficacy requirements that ensure interventions are both safe and effective for their intended uses. Informed consent processes must ensure that individuals understand the risks and benefits of enhancement interventions. Equity considerations must address how to prevent enhancement technologies from exacerbating social inequalities.

Professional and educational contexts require special consideration, as the use of cognitive enhancement in these settings raises questions about fairness and authenticity. Some contexts may require disclosure of enhancement use, while others may need to develop policies about acceptable and unacceptable forms of enhancement.

The Future Landscape of Cognitive Enhancement

Looking toward the future, cognitive enhancement technologies will likely become more sophisticated, effective, and accessible. Advances in neuroscience will enable more targeted and precise interventions, while improvements in technology will make enhancement tools more user-friendly and widely available.

The integration of cognitive enhancement with artificial intelligence and digital technologies will create new possibilities for personalized and adaptive enhancement. AI systems could monitor cognitive performance and adjust enhancement interventions in real-time, optimizing their effects for individual users and specific tasks.

However, the future of cognitive enhancement will ultimately be shaped by the choices we make about how to develop, regulate, and integrate these technologies into society. The challenge will be realizing the benefits of cognitive enhancement while addressing its risks and ensuring that its development serves human flourishing rather than creating new forms of inequality or dependency.

The cognitive enhancement revolution represents both an unprecedented opportunity and a significant responsibility. By approaching these technologies with careful consideration of their implications and commitment to human welfare, we can work toward a future where cognitive enhancement enhances rather than diminishes human potential and dignity.

In Conclusion

The future of thinking stands at a remarkable inflection point where the convergence of artificial intelligence, cognitive enhancement technologies, and our deepening understanding of human cognition is creating possibilities that were unimaginable just decades ago. We are witnessing the emergence of new forms of hybrid intelligence that combine the computational power of AI systems with the contextual understanding, creativity, and wisdom of human cognition. Simultaneously, advances in cognitive enhancement are opening new pathways for directly augmenting human mental capabilities through biochemical, physical, and behavioral interventions.

This transformation represents more than a simple technological upgrade—it constitutes a fundamental reimagining of what human cognition can become. The traditional boundaries between human and artificial intelligence are becoming increasingly fluid, creating opportunities for collaborative cognitive systems that exceed the capabilities of either humans or machines alone. The development of cognitive enhancement technologies is providing new tools for optimizing human mental performance and addressing the growing cognitive demands of modern life.

However, realizing the full potential of this cognitive revolution requires careful navigation of significant challenges and considerations. The implementation of hybrid intelligence demands not just technological sophistication but cultural transformation that preserves human agency while leveraging AI capabilities. The development of cognitive enhancement technologies must balance the promise of improved performance with concerns about safety, equity, and authenticity.

The research examined in this chapter reveals that success in this endeavor depends on several key principles. First, hybrid intelligence systems must be designed to enhance rather than replace human capabilities, preserving the essential qualities of human cognition while leveraging the computational advantages of AI systems. Second, cognitive enhancement interventions must be approached with careful attention to their multidimensional nature, recognizing that different strategies have different mechanisms, effects, and implications.

Third, the development of both hybrid intelligence and cognitive enhancement must be guided by considerations of equity and access, ensuring that the benefits of these technologies are distributed broadly rather than concentrated among privileged groups. Fourth, appropriate regulatory and ethical frameworks must be developed to guide the responsible development and deployment of cognitive technologies.

The future trajectory of human cognition will be shaped by the choices we make today about how to integrate these technologies into human life and society. The goal should not be to create cognitive systems that make humans obsolete but rather to develop technologies that amplify the best of human intelligence while preserving the qualities that make us uniquely human.

The promise of hybrid intelligence lies in its potential to create cognitive systems that are more capable, creative, and trustworthy than either humans or AI systems alone. By combining human contextual understanding, ethical reasoning, and creative insight with AI's computational power and analytical capabilities, we can address complex challenges that neither could tackle independently. This collaborative approach offers hope for solving some of the most pressing problems facing humanity while preserving human agency and dignity.

The cognitive enhancement revolution offers similar promise for directly augmenting human mental capabilities. From simple interventions like optimizing nutrition and sleep to sophisticated brain stimulation techniques and pharmaceutical interventions, these technologies could help individuals reach their full cognitive potential while addressing the growing demands of modern life. However, realizing this potential requires careful attention to safety, efficacy, and equity considerations.

Looking toward the future, we can anticipate continued advances in both hybrid intelligence and cognitive enhancement technologies. AI systems will become more sophisticated in their ability to collaborate with humans, while cognitive enhancement interventions will become more targeted, effective, and accessible. The integration of these technologies will create new possibilities for human cognitive augmentation that we are only beginning to imagine.

The challenge for the coming decades will be ensuring that this cognitive transformation serves human flourishing rather than creating new forms of dependency, inequality, or alienation. This requires ongoing dialogue between technologists, ethicists, policymakers, and society at large about how to develop and deploy cognitive technologies in ways that enhance rather than diminish human potential.

The future of thinking is not predetermined but rather emerges from the choices we make about how to design, regulate, and integrate cognitive technologies into human society. By approaching this transformation with wisdom, caution, and commitment to human welfare, we can work toward a future where technology amplifies the best of human intelligence while preserving the essential qualities that define our humanity.

The cognitive revolution we are witnessing represents both an unprecedented opportunity and a profound responsibility. The decisions we make about hybrid intelligence and cognitive enhancement will shape not only how we think and work but how we understand ourselves as human beings in an increasingly AI-augmented world. The future of thinking depends on our ability to navigate this transformation thoughtfully and deliberately, ensuring that the remarkable cognitive capabilities we are developing serve to enhance rather than replace the irreplaceable qualities of human consciousness and creativity.

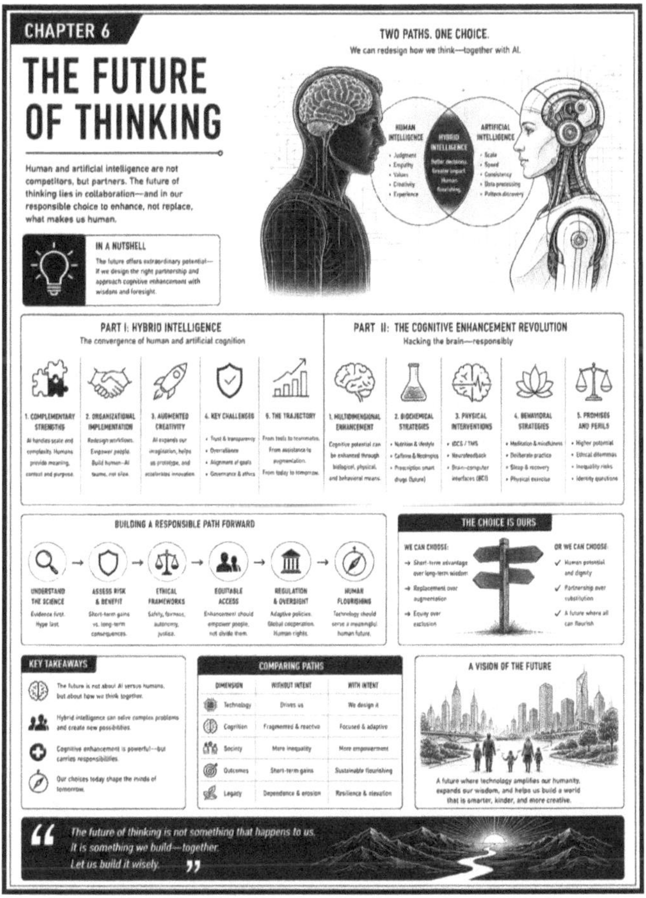

CHAPTER 6
THE FUTURE OF THINKING
Human and artificial intelligence are not competitors, but partners. The future of thinking lies in collaboration—and in our responsible choice to enhance, not replace, what makes us human.
IN A NUTSHELL
The future offers extraordinary potential—if we design the right partnership and approach cognitive enhancement with wisdom and foresight.
TWO PATHS. ONE CHOICE.
We can redesign how we think—together with AI.
HUMAN INTELLIGENCE
• Judgment
• Empathy
• Values
• Creativity
• Experience
HYBRID INTELLIGENCE
ARTIFICIAL INTELLIGENCE
• Scale
• Speed
• Consistency
• Data processing
• Pattern discovery
PART I: HYBRID INTELLIGENCE
The convergence of human and artificial cognition
1. COMPLEMENTARY STRENGTHS
AI handles scale and complexity. Humans provide meaning, context and purpose.
2. ORGANIZATIONAL IMPLEMENTATION
Redesign workflows. Empower people. Build human–AI teams, not silos.
3. AUGMENTED CREATIVITY
AI expands our imagination, helps us prototype, and accelerates innovation.
4. KEY CHALLENGES
• Trust & transparency
• Overreliance
• Alignment of goals
• Governance & ethics
5. THE TRAJECTORY
From tools to teammates. From assistance to augmentation. From today to tomorrow.
PART II: THE COGNITIVE ENHANCEMENT REVOLUTION
Hacking the brain—responsibly
1. MULTIDIMENSIONAL ENHANCEMENT
Cognitive potential can be enhanced through biological, physical, and behavioral means.
2. BIOCHEMICAL STRATEGIES
• Nutrition & lifestyle
• Caffeine & Nootropics
• Prescription smart drugs (future)
3. PHYSICAL INTERVENTIONS
• tDCS / TMS
• Neurofeedback
• Brain–computer interfaces (BCI)
4. BEHAVIORAL STRATEGIES
• Meditation & mindfulness
• Deliberate practice
• Sleep & recovery
• Physical exercise
5. PROMISES AND PERILS
• Higher potential
• Ethical dilemmas
• Inequality risks
• Identity questions
BUILDING A RESPONSIBLE PATH FORWARD
UNDERSTAND THE SCIENCE
Evidence first. Hype last.
ASSESS RISK & BENEFIT
Short-term gains vs. long-term consequences.
ETHICAL FRAMEWORKS
Safety, fairness, autonomy, justice.
EQUITABLE ACCESS
Enhancement should empower people, not divide them.
REGULATION & OVERSIGHT
Adaptive policies. Global cooperation. Human rights.
HUMAN FLOURISHING
Technology should serve a meaningful human future.
THE CHOICE IS OURS
WE CAN CHOOSE:
→ Short-term advantage over long-term wisdom
→ Replacement over augmentation
→ Equity over exclusion
OR WE CAN CHOOSE:
✓ Human potential and dignity
✓ Partnership over substitution
✓ A future where all can flourish
KEY TAKEAWAYS
The future is not about AI versus humans, but about how we think together.
Hybrid intelligence can solve complex problems and create new possibilities.
Cognitive enhancement is powerful—but carries responsibilities.
Our choices today shape the minds of tomorrow.
COMPARING PATHS
DIMENSION
WITHOUT INTENT
WITH INTENT
Technology
Drives us
We design it
Cognition
Fragmented & reactive
Focused & adaptive
Society
More inequality
More empowerment
Outcomes
Short-term gains
Sustainable flourishing
Legacy
Dependence & erosion
Resilience & elevation
A VISION OF THE FUTURE
A future where technology amplifies our humanity, expands our wisdom, and helps us build a world that is smarter, kinder, and more creative.
"The future of thinking is not something that happens to us.
It is something we build—together.
Let us build it wisely."

REFERENCES

[1] Walther, C. C. (2025, March 11). Why hybrid intelligence is the future of human-AI collaboration. *Knowledge at Wharton*. https://knowledge.wharton.upenn.edu/article/why-hybrid-intelligence-is-the-future-of-human-ai-collaboration/

[2] Dresler, M., Sandberg, A., Bublitz, C., Ohla, K., Trenado, C., Mroczko-Wąsowicz, A., Kühn, S., & Repantis, D. (2018). Hacking the brain: Dimensions of cognitive enhancement. *ACS Chemical Neuroscience*, 10(3), 1137-1148. https://pmc.ncbi.nlm.nih.gov/articles/PMC6429408/

Chapter 7: Navigating the Prompted Mind

In the preceding chapters, we have explored how artificial intelligence is transforming human cognition, creating illusions of understanding, and reshaping the very foundations of how we think and know. We have examined the biases embedded in AI systems, the neuroplastic changes occurring in our brains, and the emerging possibilities for hybrid intelligence and cognitive enhancement. Now we turn to perhaps the most practical and urgent question: How do we navigate this new cognitive landscape with wisdom and intention?

The "prompted mind" represents the contemporary human condition—a state of consciousness that is increasingly shaped by interactions with artificial intelligence systems. Every time we ask a question to a search engine, engage with a chatbot, or rely on algorithmic recommendations, we are participating in a form of cognitive collaboration that influences not only what we know but how we think. This collaboration is so pervasive and seamless that it often occurs below the threshold of conscious awareness, making it all the more important to develop strategies for navigating it thoughtfully.

The challenge of navigating the prompted mind is not simply a matter of learning to use AI tools effectively, though that is certainly important. Rather, it requires developing what we might call "cognitive sovereignty"—the ability to maintain agency and intentionality in our thinking while benefiting from the cognitive augmentation that AI systems provide. This involves understanding how AI systems influence our cognition, developing strategies for preserving essential human capabilities, and learning to collaborate with AI in ways that enhance rather than diminish our cognitive autonomy.

This chapter provides a practical framework for navigating the prompted mind in both personal and professional contexts. We will explore strategies for maintaining cognitive independence while leveraging AI capabilities, techniques for developing critical thinking skills in an AI-augmented world, and approaches for designing human-AI interactions that preserve human agency and wisdom. We will also examine the emerging field of "AI literacy" and its importance for functioning effectively in an increasingly AI-mediated world.

The central argument of this chapter is that successful navigation of the prompted mind requires active, intentional engagement with AI systems rather than passive consumption of their outputs. This means developing the skills and awareness necessary to understand how AI systems work, recognizing their limitations and biases, and maintaining the cognitive capabilities that complement rather than compete with artificial intelligence. The goal is not to resist or avoid AI systems but to engage with them in ways that enhance human flourishing and preserve the essential qualities of human consciousness.

The stakes of this navigation are high. The choices we make about how to interact with AI systems will shape not only our individual cognitive development but the broader trajectory of human consciousness in an AI-augmented world. By developing thoughtful approaches to AI collaboration, we can work toward a future where artificial intelligence amplifies human wisdom rather than replacing it, where cognitive augmentation enhances rather than diminishes human agency, and where the remarkable capabilities of AI serve to support rather than supplant the irreplaceable qualities of human thinking.

Developing Cognitive Sovereignty in an AI-Augmented World

Cognitive sovereignty—the ability to maintain agency and intentionality in our thinking while benefiting from AI augmentation—represents one of the most crucial skills for navigating the prompted mind. This concept goes beyond simple digital literacy to encompass a deeper understanding of how AI systems influence cognition and how to preserve essential human capabilities in an increasingly AI-mediated world.

Understanding AI Influence on Cognition

The first step in developing cognitive sovereignty is recognizing the subtle but pervasive ways that AI systems influence our thinking. Unlike traditional tools that we consciously choose to use for specific tasks, AI systems are increasingly embedded in the fabric of our daily cognitive activities. Search engines shape what information we encounter, recommendation algorithms influence what content we consume, and AI assistants affect how we formulate questions and process information.

This influence operates through several mechanisms that often remain below conscious awareness. Algorithmic filtering determines what information reaches our attention, potentially creating filter bubbles that limit our exposure to diverse perspectives. AI-generated content may subtly shape our language patterns and thought processes through repeated exposure. Predictive text and autocomplete features can influence how we express ideas and even what ideas we choose to pursue.

The challenge is that these influences are often beneficial in the short term—they make information access faster and more convenient—while potentially problematic in the long term if they lead to cognitive dependency or the atrophy of essential thinking skills. Developing cognitive sovereignty requires learning to recognize these influences and making conscious choices about when and how to engage with them.

Preserving Essential Human Capabilities

Cognitive sovereignty involves actively preserving and developing the human capabilities that complement rather than compete with AI systems. These include critical thinking skills, creative insight, emotional intelligence, ethical reasoning, and the ability to understand complex social and cultural contexts. Rather than allowing these capabilities to atrophy through disuse, we must consciously cultivate them as essential components of human-AI collaboration.

Critical thinking skills are particularly important in an AI-augmented world where information is abundant but not always reliable. This includes the ability to evaluate sources, identify biases, recognize logical fallacies, and distinguish between correlation and causation. While AI systems can assist with information gathering and analysis, the ability to think critically about that information remains a distinctly human responsibility.

Creative thinking represents another essential human capability that must be preserved and developed. While AI systems can generate novel combinations of existing ideas, human creativity involves understanding meaning, cultural context, and emotional resonance in ways that current AI systems cannot match. Maintaining and developing creative capabilities requires regular practice and engagement with creative challenges that go beyond what AI systems can provide.

Emotional intelligence and social cognition remain uniquely human domains that are crucial for navigating complex interpersonal and social situations. These capabilities involve understanding emotions, motivations, and social dynamics in ways that require lived experience and cultural understanding. Preserving these capabilities requires continued engagement with real human relationships and social contexts.

Strategies for Intentional AI Engagement

Developing cognitive sovereignty requires moving from passive consumption of AI outputs to active, intentional engagement with AI systems. This involves understanding how to frame questions effectively, how to interpret and validate AI responses, and how to integrate AI insights with human judgment and experience.

Effective question formulation is a crucial skill for AI interaction. This involves learning to ask questions that leverage AI capabilities while maintaining human oversight and judgment. Rather than simply accepting the first response an AI system provides, skilled users learn to ask follow-up questions, request alternative perspectives, and probe the reasoning behind AI recommendations.

Response validation represents another essential skill for AI interaction. This involves developing the ability to critically evaluate AI outputs, checking them against other sources, and understanding their limitations and potential biases. Skilled AI users learn to treat AI responses as starting points for further investigation rather than definitive answers.

Integration of AI insights with human judgment requires understanding how to combine the analytical capabilities of AI systems with human wisdom, experience, and contextual understanding. This involves learning when to trust AI recommendations, when to override them, and how to use AI analysis to inform rather than replace human decision-making.

Practical Frameworks for Human-AI Collaboration

Successful navigation of the prompted mind requires practical frameworks that guide how we interact with AI systems in various contexts. These frameworks should preserve human agency while leveraging AI capabilities, ensuring that human-AI collaboration enhances rather than diminishes human cognitive capabilities.

The CARE Framework for AI Interaction

One useful framework for AI interaction can be summarized by the acronym CARE: Clarify, Analyze, Reflect, and Evaluate. This framework provides a structured approach to AI engagement that maintains human oversight and critical thinking throughout the process.

It involves clearly defining the problem or question before engaging with AI systems. This step ensures that AI interactions are purposeful and goal-directed rather than aimless browsing or passive consumption. Clarification includes understanding what type of information or assistance is needed, what the constraints and requirements are, and what the intended use of AI outputs will be.

It involves critically examining AI responses and recommendations. This includes understanding how the AI system generated its response, what data and assumptions it relied on, and what its limitations might be. Analysis also involves comparing AI outputs with other sources and perspectives to develop a more complete understanding of the issue.

It involves considering the broader implications and context of AI recommendations. This step engages uniquely human capabilities such as ethical reasoning, cultural understanding, and long-term thinking. Reflection considers not just whether an AI recommendation is technically correct but whether it is appropriate, ethical, and aligned with human values and goals.

It involves making final judgments about how to use AI insights and recommendations. This step preserves human agency by ensuring that humans make the ultimate decisions about how to act on AI information. Evaluation considers both the technical merits of AI recommendations and their broader implications for human welfare and flourishing.

Context-Specific Strategies

Different contexts require different approaches to human-AI collaboration. Professional contexts may require more rigorous validation and documentation of AI use, while personal contexts may allow for more experimental and exploratory approaches. Educational contexts require special attention to preserving learning and development opportunities for human students.

In professional contexts, AI collaboration should be guided by principles of transparency, accountability, and quality assurance. This may involve documenting AI use, validating AI recommendations through multiple sources, and maintaining clear human oversight of important decisions. Professional contexts also require attention to ethical considerations such as bias, fairness, and the potential impact of AI recommendations on stakeholders.

Educational contexts require careful balance between leveraging AI capabilities and preserving learning opportunities for students. AI can be a powerful tool for personalized learning and educational support, but it should not replace the cognitive development that comes from struggling with challenging problems and developing independent thinking skills. Educational AI use should focus on scaffolding learning rather than providing easy answers.

Personal contexts allow for more experimental approaches to AI collaboration, but they still require attention to the long-term effects of AI use on cognitive development and well-being. Personal AI use should be guided by goals of cognitive enhancement rather than cognitive replacement, focusing on how AI can support personal growth and development rather than creating dependency.

Building AI Literacy

Effective navigation of the prompted mind requires developing AI literacy—a comprehensive understanding of how AI systems work, what their capabilities and limitations are, and how to interact with them effectively. AI literacy goes beyond technical knowledge to encompass understanding of the social, ethical, and cognitive implications of AI systems.

Technical AI literacy involves understanding the basic principles of how AI systems work, including machine learning, neural networks, and natural language processing. This knowledge helps users understand why AI systems behave as they do and what their limitations might be. Technical literacy also includes understanding concepts such as training data, bias, and uncertainty that affect AI performance.

Critical AI literacy involves developing the ability to critically evaluate AI systems and their outputs. This includes understanding how to identify potential biases, recognize limitations, and evaluate the reliability of AI recommendations. Critical literacy also involves understanding the broader social and economic forces that shape AI development and deployment.

Ethical AI literacy involves understanding the ethical implications of AI use and development. This includes awareness of issues such as privacy, fairness, accountability, and the potential impact of AI systems on society. Ethical literacy helps users make responsible decisions about when and how to use AI systems.

Practical AI literacy involves developing the skills necessary to interact effectively with AI systems. This includes learning how to formulate effective prompts, interpret AI responses, and integrate AI insights with human judgment. Practical literacy also involves understanding how to troubleshoot AI interactions and when to seek human assistance.

Preserving Human Agency in AI-Mediated Decisions

One of the most critical aspects of navigating the prompted mind involves preserving human agency in decisions that are increasingly mediated by AI systems. As AI becomes more sophisticated and pervasive, there is a risk that human decision-making could become overly dependent on AI recommendations, leading to a loss of autonomy and critical thinking skills.

Understanding Decision Automation vs. Decision Support

A crucial distinction in AI-mediated decision-making is between decision automation and decision support. Decision automation involves AI systems making decisions independently with minimal human oversight, while decision support involves AI systems providing information and analysis to support human decision-making. Understanding this distinction is essential for preserving human agency.

Decision automation may be appropriate for routine, low-stakes decisions where human oversight adds little value. Examples might include automated scheduling, basic data processing, or simple optimization tasks. However, decision automation becomes problematic when applied to complex, high-stakes, or value-laden decisions that require human judgment, ethical reasoning, or contextual understanding.

Decision support, by contrast, preserves human agency by keeping humans in the decision-making loop while leveraging AI capabilities for information processing and analysis. This approach allows humans to benefit from AI's computational advantages while maintaining responsibility for final decisions. Effective decision support systems provide transparency about their reasoning and limitations, enabling humans to make informed judgments about how to use AI recommendations.

Maintaining Critical Distance

Preserving human agency requires maintaining critical distance from AI recommendations—the ability to step back and evaluate AI outputs objectively rather than accepting them uncritically. This involves developing what researchers call "appropriate reliance" on AI systems—trusting them when they are reliable and overriding them when they are not.

Maintaining critical distance requires understanding the limitations and potential biases of AI systems. This includes awareness of how training data affects AI performance, how different contexts may affect reliability, and how AI systems may fail in unexpected ways. Critical distance also involves maintaining alternative sources of information and perspective that can provide checks on AI recommendations.

Regular practice of decision-making without AI assistance can help maintain critical distance and preserve independent thinking skills. This might involve periodically making decisions using only human judgment, seeking out diverse perspectives beyond AI recommendations, or deliberately challenging AI suggestions to test their validity.

Designing Human-Centered AI Interactions

Preserving human agency requires designing AI interactions that prioritize human autonomy and decision-making authority. This involves creating interfaces and workflows that keep humans actively engaged in cognitive processes rather than relegating them to passive recipients of AI outputs.

Human-centered AI design emphasizes transparency, explainability, and user control. AI systems should provide clear information about how they generate recommendations, what data they rely on, and what their limitations are. Users should have control over AI behavior and the ability to customize AI interactions to match their preferences and needs.

Effective human-centered design also provides multiple options and perspectives rather than single recommendations. This encourages users to consider alternatives and make active choices rather than simply accepting AI suggestions. Design should also include mechanisms for feedback and learning that allow both humans and AI systems to improve their collaboration over time.

In Conclusion

Navigating the prompted mind requires developing new skills and awareness that enable us to collaborate effectively with AI systems while preserving essential human capabilities and agency. This involves understanding how AI systems influence cognition, developing strategies for intentional AI engagement, and creating frameworks for human-AI collaboration that enhance rather than diminish human cognitive sovereignty.

The CARE framework—Clarify, Analyze, Reflect, and Evaluate—provides a practical approach to AI interaction that maintains human oversight and critical thinking throughout the process. Building comprehensive AI literacy enables more effective and responsible AI use, while preserving human agency requires maintaining critical distance from AI recommendations and designing human-centered AI interactions.

The goal is not to resist or avoid AI systems but to engage with them thoughtfully and intentionally in ways that support human flourishing. By developing cognitive sovereignty and practical frameworks for AI collaboration, we can work toward a future where artificial intelligence amplifies human wisdom rather than replacing it, where cognitive augmentation enhances rather than diminishes human agency, and where the remarkable capabilities of AI serve to support the irreplaceable qualities of human thinking.

The challenge of navigating the prompted mind will only grow more complex as AI systems become more sophisticated and pervasive. However, by developing the skills and awareness outlined in this chapter, we can approach this challenge with confidence and intention, ensuring that our collaboration with AI systems enhances rather than diminishes our humanity.

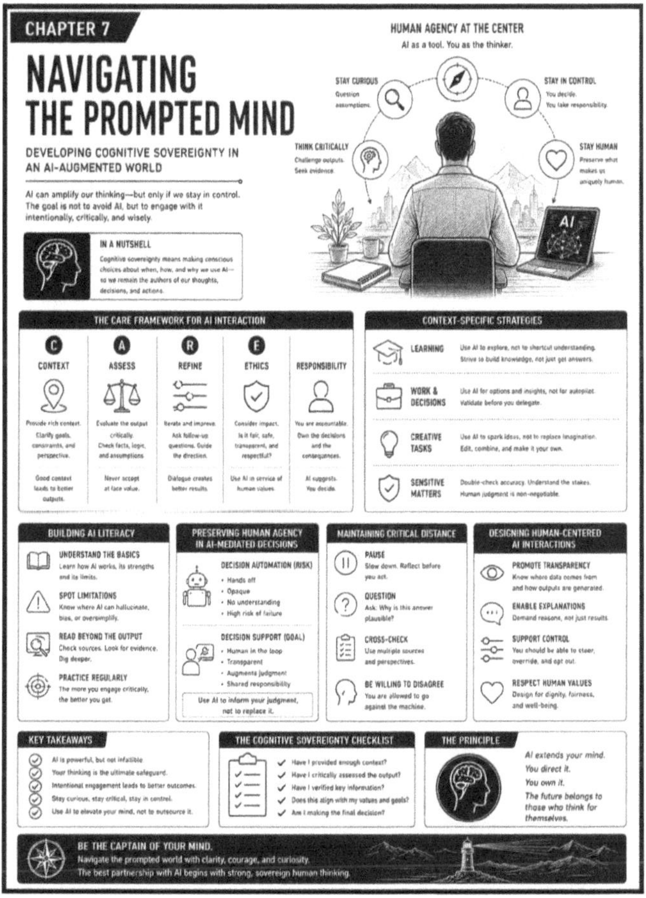
CHAPTER 7
NAVIGATING THE PROMPTED MIND
DEVELOPING COGNITIVE SOVEREIGNTY IN AN AI-AUGMENTED WORLD
AI can amplify our thinking—but only if we stay in control. The goal is not to avoid AI, but to engage with it intentionally, critically, and wisely.
IN A NUTSHELL
Cognitive sovereignty means making conscious choices about when, how, and why we use AI—so we remain the authors of our thoughts, decisions, and actions.
HUMAN AGENCY AT THE CENTER
AI as a tool. You as the thinker.
STAY CURIOUS
Question assumptions.
STAY IN CONTROL
You decide. You take responsibility.
THINK CRITICALLY
Challenge outputs. Seek evidence.
STAY HUMAN
Preserve what makes us uniquely human.
AI
THE CARE FRAMEWORK FOR AI INTERACTION
C CONTEXT
Provide rich context. Clarify goals, constraints, and perspective.
Good context leads to better outputs.
A ASSESS
Evaluate the output critically. Check facts, logic, and assumptions.
Never accept at face value.
R REFINE
Iterate and improve. Ask follow-up questions. Guide the direction.
Dialogue creates better results.
E ETHICS
Consider impact. Is it fair, safe, transparent, and respectful?
Use AI in service of human values.
RESPONSIBILITY
You are accountable. Own the decisions and the consequences.
AI suggests. You decide.
CONTEXT-SPECIFIC STRATEGIES
LEARNING
Use AI to explore, not to shortcut understanding. Strive to build knowledge, not just get answers.
WORK & DECISIONS
Use AI for options and insights, not for autopilot. Validate before you delegate.
CREATIVE TASKS
Use AI to spark ideas, not to replace imagination. Edit, combine, and make it your own.
SENSITIVE MATTERS
Double-check accuracy. Understand the stakes. Human judgment is non-negotiable.
BUILDING AI LITERACY
UNDERSTAND THE BASICS
Learn how AI works, its strengths and its limits.
SPOT LIMITATIONS
Know where AI can hallucinate, bias, or oversimplify.
READ BEYOND THE OUTPUT
Check sources. Look for evidence. Dig deeper.
PRACTICE REGULARLY
The more you engage critically, the better you get.
PRESERVING HUMAN AGENCY IN AI-MEDIATED DECISIONS
DECISION AUTOMATION (RISK)
• Hands off
• Opaque
• No understanding
• High risk of failure
DECISION SUPPORT (GOAL)
• Human in the loop
• Transparent
• Augments judgment
• Shared responsibility
Use AI to inform your judgment, not to replace it.
MAINTAINING CRITICAL DISTANCE
PAUSE
Slow down. Reflect before you act.
QUESTION
Ask: Why is this answer plausible?
CROSS-CHECK
Use multiple sources and perspectives.
BE WILLING TO DISAGREE
You are allowed to go against the machine.
DESIGNING HUMAN-CENTERED AI INTERACTIONS
PROMOTE TRANSPARENCY
Know where data comes from and how outputs are generated.
ENABLE EXPLANATIONS
Demand reasons, not just results.
SUPPORT CONTROL
You should be able to steer, override, and opt out.
RESPECT HUMAN VALUES
Design for dignity, fairness, and well-being.
KEY TAKEAWAYS
AI is powerful, but not infallible.
Your thinking is the ultimate safeguard.
Intentional engagement leads to better outcomes.
Stay curious, stay critical, stay in control.
Use AI to elevate your mind, not to outsource it.
THE COGNITIVE SOVEREIGNTY CHECKLIST
Have I provided enough context?
Have I critically assessed the output?
Have I verified key information?
Does this align with my values and goals?
Am I making the final decision?
THE PRINCIPLE
AI extends your mind.
You direct it.
You own it.
The future belongs to those who think for themselves.
BE THE CAPTAIN OF YOUR MIND.
Navigate the prompted world with clarity, courage, and curiosity.
The best partnership with AI begins with strong, sovereign human thinking.

Chapter 8: Implications for Education and Society

The cognitive transformation we have explored throughout this book extends far beyond individual psychology to encompass fundamental questions about how we organize education, structure society, and prepare future generations for an AI-augmented world. The emergence of prompted minds—human consciousness increasingly shaped by AI interaction—requires us to rethink basic assumptions about learning, knowledge, and social organization that have guided human civilization for centuries.

Educational systems designed around the assumption that students need to memorize large amounts of factual information are being challenged by a world where such information is instantly accessible through AI systems. Social structures built on traditional models of expertise and authority are being disrupted by AI systems that can provide sophisticated analysis and recommendations on virtually any topic. Economic systems based on human cognitive labor are being transformed by AI capabilities that can perform many cognitive tasks more efficiently than humans.

These changes are not merely technological upgrades to existing systems but fundamental disruptions that require new approaches to education, governance, and social organization. The challenge is not simply adapting to AI but reimagining human institutions in ways that leverage AI capabilities while preserving essential human values and capabilities. This requires understanding how AI transformation affects different aspects of society and developing strategies for managing this transition thoughtfully and equitably.

This chapter examines the broad social implications of the cognitive transformation we have explored throughout this book. We will investigate how educational systems must evolve to prepare students for an AI-augmented world, how social institutions need to adapt to the realities of human-AI collaboration, and how we can ensure that the benefits of cognitive transformation are distributed equitably across society.

We will also explore the challenges and opportunities created by AI transformation for different groups and communities, examining how factors such as age, education, and socioeconomic status affect people's ability to navigate the prompted mind. The goal is to understand not just how AI is changing individual cognition but how these changes are reshaping the broader social fabric and what this means for human flourishing.

The central argument of this chapter is that successfully managing the social implications of AI transformation requires proactive, intentional efforts to redesign human institutions in ways that leverage AI capabilities while preserving human agency, equity, and social cohesion. This is not a challenge that can be left to market forces or technological determinism but requires deliberate social and political action to ensure that AI transformation serves human welfare rather than undermining it.

Reimagining Education for the AI Age

The transformation of human cognition by AI systems requires a fundamental reimagining of educational systems that have remained largely unchanged for centuries. Traditional educational models, designed around the assumption that students need to acquire and retain large amounts of factual information, are being challenged by a world where such information is instantly accessible through AI systems. This shift requires new approaches to learning that emphasize skills and capabilities that complement rather than compete with AI.

From Information Transfer to Cognitive Development

The traditional model of education as information transfer—where teachers transmit knowledge to students who memorize and reproduce it—is becoming increasingly obsolete in an AI-augmented world. When factual information is instantly accessible through AI systems, the value of memorized knowledge diminishes relative to skills such as critical thinking, creative problem-solving, and the ability to work effectively with AI tools.

This shift requires moving from a focus on what students know to how they think. Rather than emphasizing the acquisition of factual knowledge, education must focus on developing cognitive capabilities that enable students to navigate complex, ambiguous situations and to collaborate effectively with AI systems. This includes skills such as asking good questions, evaluating information critically, synthesizing insights from multiple sources, and making ethical judgments about complex issues.

The challenge is that these higher-order thinking skills are more difficult to teach and assess than factual knowledge. They require experiential learning, practice with real-world problems, and the development of judgment that comes from engaging with complex, ambiguous situations. Educational systems must develop new pedagogical approaches that can effectively cultivate these capabilities while still providing students with the foundational knowledge they need to think effectively.

Developing AI Literacy as a Core Competency

One of the most crucial educational needs in an AI-augmented world is the development of AI literacy as a core competency for all students. AI literacy goes beyond technical knowledge about how AI systems work to encompass understanding of how to interact with AI effectively, how to evaluate AI outputs critically, and how to maintain human agency in AI-mediated environments.

Technical AI literacy involves understanding the basic principles of machine learning, neural networks, and natural language processing. Students need to understand concepts such as training data, bias, and uncertainty that affect AI performance. This knowledge helps students understand why AI systems behave as they do and what their limitations might be.

Critical AI literacy involves developing the ability to evaluate AI systems and their outputs critically. This includes understanding how to identify potential biases, recognize limitations, and assess the reliability of AI recommendations. Students need to learn how to fact-check AI outputs, seek alternative perspectives, and maintain healthy skepticism about AI claims.

Ethical AI literacy involves understanding the ethical implications of AI development and use. Students need to understand issues such as privacy, fairness, accountability, and the potential impact of AI systems on society. This includes developing the ability to make ethical judgments about when and how to use AI systems.

Practical AI literacy involves developing the skills necessary to interact effectively with AI systems. This includes learning how to formulate effective prompts, interpret AI responses, and integrate AI insights with human judgment. Students need hands-on experience working with AI tools in various contexts to develop fluency in human-AI collaboration.

Preserving Essential Human Capabilities

While developing AI literacy is crucial, education must also focus on preserving and developing the essential human capabilities that complement AI systems. These include creative thinking, emotional intelligence, ethical reasoning, and the ability to understand complex social and cultural contexts. Rather than allowing these capabilities to atrophy through over-reliance on AI, educational systems must actively cultivate them as essential components of human development.

Creative thinking remains a uniquely human capability that involves understanding meaning, cultural context, and emotional resonance in ways that current AI systems cannot match. Educational approaches that foster creativity include project-based learning, artistic expression, and open-ended problem-solving that encourages students to develop original ideas and approaches.

Emotional intelligence and social cognition are crucial for navigating complex interpersonal and social situations. Educational programs must continue to emphasize the development of empathy, communication skills, and the ability to understand and work with diverse groups of people. This requires experiential learning through group projects, community engagement, and real-world problem-solving.

Ethical reasoning becomes increasingly important in a world where AI systems can provide sophisticated analysis but lack the moral judgment necessary for making ethical decisions. Students need opportunities to grapple with complex ethical dilemmas, understand different ethical frameworks, and develop the ability to make principled decisions in ambiguous situations.

Personalized and Adaptive Learning

AI systems offer unprecedented opportunities for personalizing education to meet individual student needs and learning styles. AI-powered educational technologies can adapt to student progress, provide customized feedback, and identify areas where students need additional support. However, implementing personalized learning effectively requires careful attention to preserving human agency and avoiding over-dependence on AI systems.

Effective personalized learning uses AI to support rather than replace human teachers and human learning processes. AI can help identify student needs, suggest learning resources, and provide feedback on student work, but human teachers remain essential for providing mentorship, emotional support, and the kind of contextual understanding that AI systems lack.

Personalized learning also requires attention to equity and access. While AI-powered educational technologies can provide sophisticated support for learning, they may also exacerbate existing inequalities if they are not made available to all students. Educational systems must ensure that the benefits of AI-enhanced learning are distributed equitably rather than concentrated among privileged groups.

Social Transformation and Institutional Adaptation

The cognitive transformation brought about by AI systems extends beyond education to affect virtually every aspect of social organization. Institutions designed around traditional models of human cognition and expertise must adapt to the realities of human-AI collaboration while preserving essential human values and social functions.

Redefining Expertise and Authority

Traditional models of expertise based on the accumulation and retention of specialized knowledge are being challenged by AI systems that can provide sophisticated analysis and recommendations across virtually any domain. This shift requires rethinking how we understand and organize expertise in professional and social contexts.

Rather than being defined by what they know, experts in an AI-augmented world are increasingly defined by their ability to work effectively with AI systems while providing the contextual understanding, ethical judgment, and creative insight that AI systems lack. This includes the ability to formulate good questions for AI systems, critically evaluate AI outputs, and integrate AI insights with human wisdom and experience.

Professional education and credentialing systems must adapt to this new reality by focusing on developing the skills necessary for effective human-AI collaboration rather than simply testing factual knowledge. This includes developing assessment methods that can evaluate critical thinking, ethical reasoning, and the ability to work effectively with AI tools.

The democratization of access to sophisticated analysis through AI systems also raises questions about traditional hierarchies of expertise and authority. When anyone can access AI-powered analysis on complex topics, the basis for expert authority shifts from exclusive access to information toward the ability to interpret and contextualize that information effectively.

Governance and Decision-Making in an AI-Augmented World

The integration of AI systems into governance and decision-making processes offers opportunities for more informed and efficient public administration while raising concerns about accountability, transparency, and democratic participation. AI systems can analyze vast amounts of data to inform policy decisions, predict the outcomes of different policy options, and identify patterns that human analysts might miss.

However, the use of AI in governance also raises fundamental questions about democratic accountability and human agency in public decision-making. When AI systems influence or make decisions that affect people's lives, ensuring appropriate human oversight and accountability becomes crucial. This requires developing new frameworks for AI governance that preserve democratic values while leveraging AI capabilities.

Transparency and explainability become particularly important in governmental AI applications. Citizens have a right to understand how decisions that affect them are made, including the role that AI systems play in those decisions. This requires AI systems that can provide clear explanations of their reasoning and decision-making processes.

Public participation in AI governance is also crucial for ensuring that AI systems serve the public interest rather than narrow technical or commercial interests. This includes involving diverse stakeholders in the design and oversight of governmental AI systems and ensuring that the benefits and risks of AI are distributed equitably across society.

Economic Implications and Workforce Transformation

The cognitive transformation brought about by AI systems has profound implications for economic organization and workforce development. As AI systems become capable of performing an increasing range of cognitive tasks, the nature of human work is being fundamentally transformed. This creates both opportunities for enhanced productivity and creativity and challenges related to job displacement and economic inequality.

The key to managing this transformation successfully is focusing on human-AI collaboration rather than human-AI competition. Rather than simply replacing human workers with AI systems, the goal should be to create hybrid work environments that leverage the complementary strengths of humans and AI. This requires rethinking job design, workplace organization, and workforce development to support effective human-AI collaboration.

Workforce development programs must evolve to prepare workers for an AI-augmented economy. This includes developing AI literacy skills, fostering the human capabilities that complement AI systems, and providing ongoing education and training to help workers adapt to changing technological capabilities. The goal is to ensure that workers can thrive in an AI-augmented economy rather than being displaced by it.

Economic policies must also address the potential for AI transformation to exacerbate existing inequalities. If the benefits of AI are concentrated among those who own AI technologies or have the skills to work with them effectively, AI transformation could increase rather than decrease economic inequality. Addressing this challenge requires policies that ensure broad access to AI technologies and the education necessary to use them effectively.

Social Cohesion and Cultural Preservation

The transformation of human cognition by AI systems raises important questions about social cohesion and cultural preservation. As AI systems increasingly mediate human communication and information access, there is a risk that shared cultural knowledge and social bonds could be weakened. AI-powered filter bubbles and echo chambers could fragment society into isolated groups with little common understanding or shared experience.

Preserving social cohesion in an AI-augmented world requires intentional efforts to maintain shared cultural knowledge and common experiences. This includes ensuring that educational systems continue to transmit cultural knowledge and values, that media systems provide opportunities for shared cultural experiences, and that AI systems are designed to promote rather than undermine social connection.

Cultural preservation also requires attention to how AI systems represent and transmit cultural knowledge. AI systems trained primarily on dominant cultural perspectives may marginalize or misrepresent minority cultures and perspectives. Ensuring cultural diversity and representation in AI systems requires deliberate efforts to include diverse voices and perspectives in AI development and training.

The challenge is balancing the benefits of AI-powered personalization and efficiency with the need for shared cultural experiences and social cohesion. This requires designing AI systems that can provide personalized experiences while also promoting exposure to diverse perspectives and maintaining connections to broader cultural and social contexts.

Equity and Access in the AI Age

One of the most critical challenges in managing the social implications of AI transformation is ensuring that the benefits of AI are distributed equitably across society. The risk is that AI transformation could exacerbate existing inequalities by providing advantages to those who have access to AI technologies and the skills to use them effectively while leaving others behind.

The Digital Divide in an AI World

The traditional digital divide—the gap between those who have access to digital technologies and those who do not—is being transformed and potentially exacerbated by AI technologies. While basic internet access and digital literacy remain important, the new digital divide increasingly centers on access to sophisticated AI tools and the skills necessary to use them effectively.

This new AI divide has multiple dimensions. Economic factors affect access to advanced AI tools and services, which may be expensive or require significant computational resources. Educational factors affect the ability to develop AI literacy and the skills necessary for effective human-AI collaboration. Cultural and linguistic factors affect how well AI systems work for different groups, as many AI systems are optimized for dominant languages and cultural contexts.

Addressing the AI divide requires comprehensive efforts to ensure equitable access to AI technologies and education. This includes public investment in AI infrastructure and education, policies that promote competition and affordability in AI markets, and efforts to ensure that AI systems work effectively for diverse populations and use cases.

Inclusive AI Development and Deployment

Ensuring equity in the AI age requires attention to how AI systems are developed and deployed. AI systems that are developed primarily by and for privileged groups may not work effectively for or may even harm marginalized communities. Inclusive AI development requires diverse teams, diverse training data, and attention to how AI systems affect different groups.

Diverse development teams bring different perspectives and experiences that can help identify potential biases and limitations in AI systems. This includes diversity across dimensions such as race, gender, age, disability status, and socioeconomic background. Diverse teams are more likely to identify potential problems and develop solutions that work for diverse populations.

Diverse training data is crucial for ensuring that AI systems work effectively for different groups. AI systems trained primarily on data from dominant groups may not work well for marginalized communities or may perpetuate existing biases and inequalities. Ensuring diverse and representative training data requires deliberate efforts to collect data from diverse sources and populations.

Impact assessment and monitoring are essential for understanding how AI systems affect different groups and for identifying and addressing potential harms. This includes ongoing monitoring of AI system performance across different populations and regular assessment of the social and economic impacts of AI deployment.

Policy Frameworks for Equitable AI

Managing the social implications of AI transformation requires comprehensive policy frameworks that promote equity while enabling innovation and economic growth. These frameworks must address multiple dimensions of AI governance, including access, safety, accountability, and social impact.

Access policies should ensure that the benefits of AI are broadly available rather than concentrated among privileged groups. This may include public investment in AI infrastructure and education, regulations that promote competition and affordability in AI markets, and programs that provide AI access to underserved communities.

Safety and accountability policies should ensure that AI systems are safe, reliable, and accountable to the communities they affect. This includes requirements for testing and validation of AI systems, transparency and explainability requirements, and mechanisms for addressing harms caused by AI systems.

Social impact policies should address the broader social and economic effects of AI transformation. This may include workforce development programs, social safety nets for workers displaced by AI, and policies that ensure the benefits of AI-driven productivity gains are shared broadly across society.

International cooperation is also crucial for managing the global implications of AI transformation. AI technologies cross national boundaries, and their effects are felt globally. Addressing challenges such as AI safety, equity, and governance requires international cooperation and coordination.

In Conclusion

The social implications of AI transformation are vast and complex, affecting virtually every aspect of human society from education and governance to economic organization and cultural preservation. Successfully managing this transformation requires proactive, intentional efforts to redesign human institutions in ways that leverage AI capabilities while preserving human agency, equity, and social cohesion.

Educational systems must evolve from information transfer models to focus on developing the cognitive capabilities that complement AI systems, including critical thinking, creativity, and ethical reasoning. AI literacy must become a core competency for all students, while educational approaches must preserve and develop essential human capabilities.

Social institutions must adapt to the realities of human-AI collaboration while preserving democratic values and human agency. This includes rethinking expertise and authority, developing new frameworks for AI governance, and managing the economic implications of workforce transformation.

Ensuring equity in the AI age requires comprehensive efforts to address the new forms of digital divide created by AI technologies. This includes inclusive AI development, equitable access policies, and comprehensive policy frameworks that promote both innovation and social welfare.

The challenge is enormous, but so is the opportunity. By approaching AI transformation thoughtfully and deliberately, we can work toward a future where AI enhances rather than undermines human flourishing, where the benefits of cognitive augmentation are shared broadly across society, and where technology serves to strengthen rather than weaken the social bonds that hold communities together.

The choices we make about how to manage the social implications of AI transformation will shape the future of human society for generations to come. By understanding these implications and working proactively to address them, we can help ensure that the remarkable capabilities of AI serve to enhance rather than diminish human welfare and social cohesion.

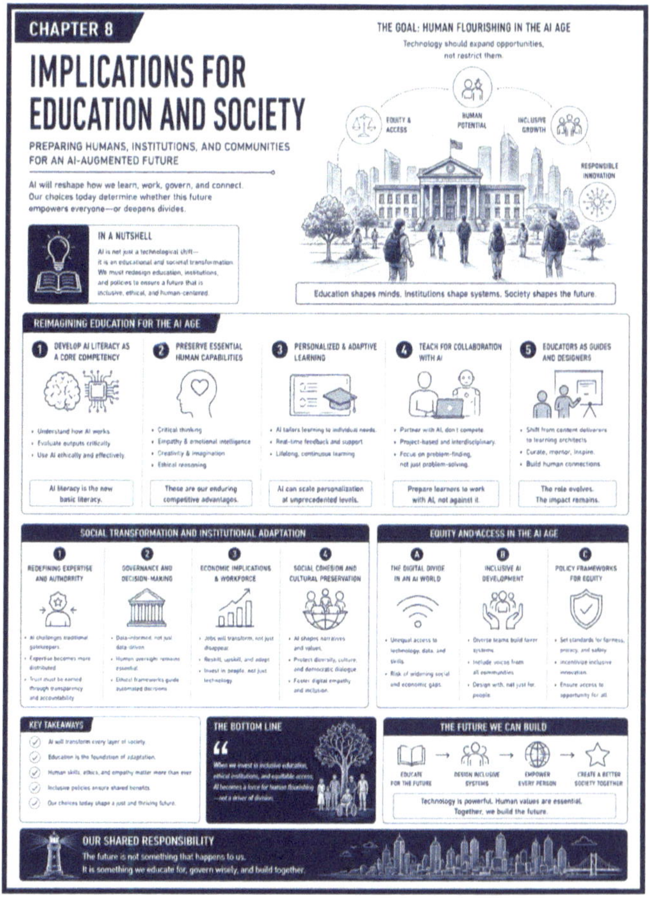

Chapter 9: Toward a New Cognitive Partnership

As we reach the conclusion of our exploration into the prompted mind, we find ourselves at a remarkable juncture in human history. The journey through the preceding chapters has revealed the profound ways in which artificial intelligence is reshaping human cognition, creating new forms of understanding while simultaneously generating illusions of comprehension. We have examined how cognitive offloading is transforming the very architecture of human thought, how biases embedded in AI systems are shaping our perceptions of reality, and how the future of thinking itself is being redefined through the convergence of human and artificial intelligence.

The picture that emerges is neither utopian nor dystopian but profoundly complex. We are witnessing the birth of a new form of cognitive partnership between humans and machines—one that offers unprecedented opportunities for enhancing human capability and understanding while simultaneously creating new risks and challenges that require careful navigation. This partnership is not optional; it is already underway, embedded in the fabric of our daily cognitive activities through search engines, recommendation systems, and AI assistants that increasingly mediate our interactions with information and knowledge.

The central question is not whether this cognitive partnership will continue to develop—it almost certainly will—but whether we can guide its evolution in directions that enhance rather than diminish human flourishing. The research and analysis presented throughout this book suggest that the answer depends on our ability to approach this partnership with wisdom, intentionality, and a deep understanding of both its possibilities and its pitfalls.

This final chapter synthesizes the key insights from our exploration and proposes a framework for moving toward a cognitive partnership that preserves the best of human intelligence while leveraging the remarkable capabilities of artificial systems. We will examine the principles that should guide this partnership, the challenges that must be addressed, and the opportunities that await if we can navigate this transformation thoughtfully and deliberately.

The central argument of this concluding chapter is that the future of human cognition lies not in competition with artificial intelligence but in collaboration—a partnership that combines the computational power and analytical capabilities of AI systems with the wisdom, creativity, and ethical judgment that define human consciousness. However, realizing this potential requires active, intentional effort to shape the development and deployment of AI technologies in ways that serve human welfare and preserve the essential qualities that make us human.

The stakes could not be higher. The choices we make about this cognitive partnership will determine not only how we think and learn but how we understand ourselves as conscious beings in an increasingly AI-augmented world. By approaching this challenge with the seriousness and thoughtfulness it deserves, we can work toward a future where artificial intelligence amplifies the best of human intelligence rather than replacing it, where cognitive augmentation enhances rather than diminishes human agency, and where the remarkable capabilities of AI serve to support the flourishing of human consciousness and creativity.

Synthesis of Key Insights

Our exploration of the prompted mind has revealed several fundamental insights about the nature of human-AI interaction and its implications for the future of human cognition. These insights provide the foundation for understanding how to approach the cognitive partnership between humans and artificial intelligence in ways that enhance rather than diminish human capability and flourishing.

The Illusion of Understanding and Its Implications

One of the most significant insights from our investigation is the pervasive nature of the illusion of understanding created by AI systems. As we explored in earlier chapters, AI systems can produce responses that appear to demonstrate deep comprehension while actually operating through sophisticated pattern matching and statistical correlation. This illusion is so convincing that it can deceive not only users but sometimes even the developers of AI systems themselves.

The implications of this illusion extend far beyond technical considerations to encompass fundamental questions about knowledge, expertise, and truth. When AI systems can provide convincing explanations and analyses across virtually any domain, traditional markers of understanding and expertise become less reliable. This creates both opportunities and risks: opportunities for democratizing access to sophisticated analysis and insights, but risks of mistaking computational processing for genuine comprehension.

Understanding this illusion is crucial for developing effective strategies for human-AI collaboration. It suggests that successful cognitive partnership requires maintaining healthy skepticism about AI outputs while still being able to leverage their analytical capabilities. This means developing the ability to distinguish between AI's computational strengths and its limitations in genuine understanding, context, and meaning-making.

The Transformation of Cognitive Architecture

Our examination of neuroplasticity and cognitive transformation has revealed that interaction with AI systems is producing measurable changes in human brain structure and function. The emergence of the "online brain" represents a fundamental reorganization of cognitive architecture in response to digital technology and AI interaction. These changes affect core cognitive processes including attention, memory, and social cognition.

This transformation is neither inherently positive nor negative but represents an adaptation to new environmental demands. The key insight is that these changes are not predetermined but can be influenced by how we design and interact with AI systems. By understanding the mechanisms of cognitive transformation, we can work to guide these changes in directions that enhance rather than diminish human cognitive capabilities.

The neuroplastic nature of human cognition also suggests that we have more agency in shaping our cognitive future than we might assume. The brain's remarkable adaptability means that conscious choices about how we engage with AI systems can influence the direction of cognitive change. This places responsibility on individuals, educators, and society to make thoughtful decisions about AI interaction and cognitive development.

The Complementary Nature of Human and Artificial Intelligence

Throughout our exploration, a consistent theme has emerged: human and artificial intelligence have fundamentally different strengths and limitations that make them naturally complementary rather than competitive. AI systems excel at processing vast amounts of data, identifying patterns, and performing rapid calculations, while humans excel at contextual understanding, ethical reasoning, creative insight, and meaning-making.

This complementarity suggests that the most effective approach to cognitive partnership involves leveraging the strengths of both humans and AI while compensating for their respective limitations. Rather than viewing AI as a replacement for human cognition, we should approach it as a powerful tool for augmenting human capabilities in areas where AI excels while preserving and developing the uniquely human capabilities that AI cannot replicate.

The challenge is designing interactions and systems that effectively combine these complementary capabilities. This requires understanding not just what each type of intelligence can do but how they can work together synergistically to produce outcomes that neither could achieve alone.

The Importance of Context and Bias Awareness

Our investigation of context and bias in AI systems has revealed the critical importance of understanding how these factors shape AI behavior and outputs. AI systems are not neutral tools but embody the biases present in their training data, design decisions, and deployment contexts. These biases can have significant impacts on AI recommendations and decisions, particularly for marginalized or underrepresented groups.

Understanding bias and context is essential for effective AI collaboration because it enables users to interpret AI outputs more accurately and to identify potential limitations or problems. This awareness also highlights the importance of diverse perspectives in AI development and the need for ongoing monitoring and adjustment of AI systems to address bias and ensure fairness.

The context problem in AI—the difficulty AI systems have in understanding and adapting to different contexts—also emphasizes the continued importance of human judgment and oversight. While AI systems can provide powerful analytical capabilities, humans remain essential for understanding context, interpreting meaning, and making decisions that require cultural, social, or ethical understanding.

Principles for Cognitive Partnership

Based on the insights from our exploration, we can identify several key principles that should guide the development of cognitive partnership between humans and artificial intelligence. These principles provide a framework for approaching AI collaboration in ways that enhance human capability while preserving essential human values and agency.

Principle 1: Augmentation Over Replacement

The first and most fundamental principle is that AI should be designed and deployed to augment rather than replace human cognitive capabilities. This means focusing on how AI can enhance human thinking, creativity, and decision-making rather than simply automating human tasks. The goal should be to create cognitive systems that make humans more capable and effective rather than making humans redundant.

Implementing this principle requires careful attention to the design of human-AI interfaces and workflows. AI systems should be designed to keep humans actively engaged in cognitive processes rather than relegating them to passive recipients of AI outputs. This includes providing transparency about AI reasoning, offering multiple options and perspectives, and maintaining meaningful human control over important decisions.

Augmentation over replacement also means preserving opportunities for human cognitive development and learning. AI systems should support rather than bypass the cognitive processes that enable humans to develop expertise, creativity, and judgment. This is particularly important in educational contexts where the goal is to develop human capabilities rather than simply provide correct answers.

Principle 2: Transparency and Explainability

Effective cognitive partnership requires AI systems that can provide clear explanations of their reasoning and decision-making processes. Users need to understand how AI systems generate their outputs, what data and assumptions they rely on, and what their limitations might be. This transparency is essential for enabling humans to make informed judgments about when and how to trust AI recommendations.

Explainability is particularly important for high-stakes decisions where AI recommendations could have significant consequences. In these contexts, humans need to be able to understand and evaluate AI reasoning to ensure that decisions are appropriate and ethical. This requires AI systems that can provide not just outputs but meaningful explanations of how those outputs were generated.

Transparency also extends to the broader context of AI development and deployment. Users should understand who developed AI systems, what their intended purposes are, and what potential biases or limitations they might have. This contextual information is crucial for interpreting AI outputs appropriately and identifying potential conflicts of interest or misaligned incentives.

Principle 3: Human Agency and Control

Cognitive partnership must preserve meaningful human agency and control over important decisions and cognitive processes. While AI systems can provide valuable analysis and recommendations, humans should retain ultimate authority over decisions that affect their lives and the lives of others. This requires designing AI systems that support rather than supplant human decision-making authority.

Maintaining human agency requires providing users with meaningful choices about how to interact with AI systems. This includes the ability to customize AI behavior, override AI recommendations, and choose when and how to engage with AI assistance. Users should not be forced into AI-mediated interactions but should have genuine alternatives that preserve their autonomy.

Human control also requires ongoing human oversight of AI systems, particularly in contexts where AI decisions could have significant impacts. This includes mechanisms for monitoring AI performance, identifying and correcting errors, and ensuring that AI systems continue to serve human values and goals over time.

Principle 4: Equity and Inclusion

The benefits of cognitive partnership should be distributed equitably across society rather than concentrated among privileged groups. This requires attention to how AI systems are developed, deployed, and made accessible to different communities. AI systems should work effectively for diverse populations and should not perpetuate or exacerbate existing inequalities.

Ensuring equity requires diverse representation in AI development teams and processes. AI systems developed primarily by and for dominant groups may not work well for marginalized communities or may even cause harm. Inclusive development processes that involve diverse stakeholders can help identify and address potential problems before they become embedded in AI systems.

Access to AI technologies and the education necessary to use them effectively is also crucial for equity. If cognitive partnership provides significant advantages, ensuring broad access to these capabilities becomes essential for preventing new forms of inequality. This may require public investment in AI infrastructure and education as well as policies that promote competition and affordability in AI markets.

Principle 5: Continuous Learning and Adaptation

Cognitive partnership is not a static relationship but an evolving collaboration that requires continuous learning and adaptation from both humans and AI systems. As AI capabilities advance and human understanding of AI deepens, the nature of the partnership will continue to evolve. This requires flexibility and openness to change from all participants in the cognitive partnership.

For humans, continuous learning means developing and maintaining AI literacy, staying informed about AI capabilities and limitations, and adapting interaction strategies as AI systems evolve. This includes both technical understanding of how AI systems work and practical skills for collaborating with AI effectively.

For AI systems, continuous learning means ongoing improvement based on feedback from human users and changing contexts. This includes mechanisms for updating AI models, addressing biases and errors, and adapting to new use cases and requirements. AI systems should be designed to learn from their interactions with humans and to improve their collaboration capabilities over time.

Challenges and Opportunities

The path toward effective cognitive partnership is not without challenges, but it also offers remarkable opportunities for enhancing human capability and addressing complex problems that neither humans nor AI could tackle alone. Understanding both the challenges and opportunities is essential for navigating this transformation successfully.

Challenges in Developing Cognitive Partnership

One of the primary challenges in developing cognitive partnership is managing the complexity of human-AI interaction. As AI systems become more sophisticated and are deployed in more contexts, the cognitive demands of managing these interactions may become overwhelming. Users need to understand multiple AI systems with different capabilities, limitations, and interaction patterns, which can create significant cognitive overhead.

Another challenge is maintaining appropriate calibration of trust in AI systems. Users need to develop "appropriate reliance"—trusting AI systems when they are reliable and overriding them when they are not. This requires sophisticated understanding of AI capabilities and limitations that may be difficult for many users to develop and maintain.

The pace of AI development also creates challenges for cognitive partnership. As AI capabilities advance rapidly, users may struggle to keep up with changing capabilities and interaction patterns. Educational systems and training programs may lag behind technological development, leaving users unprepared for new AI capabilities.

Ethical and social challenges also complicate the development of cognitive partnership. Questions about privacy, autonomy, fairness, and social impact require ongoing attention and may not have clear or stable answers. Balancing the benefits of AI collaboration with concerns about human agency and social welfare requires careful consideration and ongoing dialogue.

Opportunities for Enhanced Human Capability

Despite these challenges, cognitive partnership offers remarkable opportunities for enhancing human capability and addressing complex problems. The combination of human wisdom and creativity with AI's computational power and analytical capabilities could enable new forms of problem-solving and innovation that neither could achieve alone.

In scientific research, cognitive partnership could accelerate discovery by enabling researchers to analyze vast datasets, identify patterns across multiple domains, and generate hypotheses that might not occur to human researchers alone. AI systems could handle routine analysis while humans focus on interpretation, meaning-making, and the creative insights that drive scientific breakthroughs.

In education, cognitive partnership could enable personalized learning experiences that adapt to individual student needs while preserving the human mentorship and guidance that are essential for development. AI systems could provide customized content and feedback while human teachers focus on inspiration, motivation, and the social and emotional aspects of learning.

In creative fields, cognitive partnership could enhance human creativity by providing new sources of inspiration, enabling rapid exploration of creative possibilities, and handling routine aspects of creative work. This could free human creators to focus on the conceptual, emotional, and meaning-making aspects of creative work that define artistic and cultural value.

Building Sustainable Cognitive Partnership

Creating sustainable cognitive partnership requires ongoing attention to the balance between leveraging AI capabilities and preserving essential human qualities. This balance is not static but requires continuous adjustment as AI capabilities evolve and human understanding deepens.

Sustainability also requires attention to the long-term effects of cognitive partnership on human development and society. While AI collaboration may provide short-term benefits, we must consider its long-term impacts on human cognitive development, social relationships, and cultural transmission. This requires ongoing research and monitoring to understand how cognitive partnership affects human flourishing over time.

Building sustainable partnership also requires institutional support for the development and maintenance of cognitive partnership capabilities. This includes educational systems that prepare people for AI collaboration, regulatory frameworks that ensure AI safety and accountability, and social support systems that help people adapt to changing technological capabilities.

A Vision for the Future

As we look toward the future of cognitive partnership, we can envision a world where the collaboration between human and artificial intelligence enhances rather than diminishes human capability and flourishing. This vision is not inevitable but represents a possibility that we can work toward through thoughtful action and deliberate choice.

The Flourishing Mind in an AI-Augmented World

In this future vision, humans and AI systems work together as cognitive partners, each contributing their unique strengths to shared endeavors. Humans provide wisdom, creativity, ethical judgment, and contextual understanding, while AI systems provide computational power, pattern recognition, and analytical capabilities. Together, they tackle complex problems and create new possibilities that neither could achieve alone.

Education in this future focuses on developing the human capabilities that complement AI systems while also providing the AI literacy necessary for effective collaboration. Students learn to think critically, create meaningfully, and collaborate effectively with both humans and AI systems. The goal is not to compete with AI but to work with it in ways that enhance human potential.

Work in this future is characterized by human-AI collaboration that enhances rather than replaces human capabilities. Workers use AI tools to augment their analytical and creative capabilities while focusing on the uniquely human aspects of their roles. The result is more fulfilling work that leverages human strengths while benefiting from AI capabilities.

Society in this future is characterized by equitable access to AI technologies and the education necessary to use them effectively. The benefits of cognitive partnership are shared broadly rather than concentrated among privileged groups. AI systems are designed and deployed in ways that serve human welfare and preserve human agency and dignity.

The Path Forward

Realizing this vision requires coordinated action across multiple domains. Technologists must design AI systems that support rather than supplant human capabilities, with attention to transparency, explainability, and human control. Educators must develop new approaches to learning that prepare students for cognitive partnership while preserving essential human capabilities.

Policymakers must create regulatory frameworks that promote innovation while ensuring safety, equity, and accountability. Society as a whole must engage in ongoing dialogue about the values and goals that should guide AI development and deployment.

Individuals must take responsibility for developing their own AI literacy and cognitive partnership capabilities. This includes understanding how AI systems work, developing critical thinking skills for evaluating AI outputs, and maintaining the human capabilities that complement AI systems.

The path forward is not predetermined but emerges from the choices we make about how to develop, deploy, and interact with AI systems. By approaching cognitive partnership with wisdom, intentionality, and commitment to human welfare, we can work toward a future where artificial intelligence enhances rather than diminishes the remarkable capabilities that define human consciousness and creativity.

In Conclusion

The journey through the prompted mind has revealed both the profound challenges and remarkable opportunities created by the cognitive transformation we are experiencing. We stand at a unique moment in human history where the boundaries between human and artificial intelligence are becoming increasingly fluid, creating possibilities for cognitive partnership that were unimaginable just decades ago.

The research and analysis presented throughout this book demonstrate that this transformation is not simply a matter of adopting new tools but represents a fundamental reorganization of human cognitive architecture. The emergence of prompted minds—human consciousness increasingly shaped by AI interaction—requires us to rethink basic assumptions about thinking, learning, and knowing that have guided human civilization for millennia.

The path forward lies not in resistance to this transformation but in thoughtful engagement with it. By understanding how AI systems influence cognition, recognizing their capabilities and limitations, and developing strategies for effective collaboration, we can work toward a cognitive partnership that enhances rather than diminishes human potential.

The principles outlined in this chapter—augmentation over replacement, transparency and explainability, human agency and control, equity and inclusion, and continuous learning and adaptation—provide a framework for approaching this partnership in ways that serve human flourishing. However, realizing this potential requires ongoing effort and attention from individuals, institutions, and society as a whole.

The future of human cognition is not predetermined but emerges from the choices we make about how to develop, deploy, and interact with AI systems. By approaching cognitive partnership with wisdom, intentionality, and commitment to human welfare, we can work toward a future where artificial intelligence amplifies the best of human intelligence rather than replacing it.

The prompted mind represents both a challenge and an opportunity. The challenge is learning to navigate an increasingly AI-mediated cognitive environment while preserving the essential qualities that define human consciousness. The opportunity is creating new forms of cognitive capability that combine the best of human and artificial intelligence to address complex problems and enhance human flourishing.

As we move forward into this AI-augmented future, the responsibility lies with each of us to engage thoughtfully and deliberately with the cognitive partnership that is already emerging. By understanding the implications of this transformation and working actively to shape its direction, we can help ensure that the remarkable capabilities of artificial intelligence serve to enhance rather than diminish the irreplaceable qualities of human consciousness, creativity, and wisdom.

The future of thinking depends on our ability to navigate this transformation with the seriousness and thoughtfulness it deserves. The choices we make today about cognitive partnership will shape not only how we think and learn but how we understand ourselves as conscious beings in an increasingly AI-augmented world. By approaching this challenge with wisdom and commitment to human flourishing, we can work toward a future where the prompted mind represents not a diminishment of human capability but its enhancement and expansion into new realms of possibility.

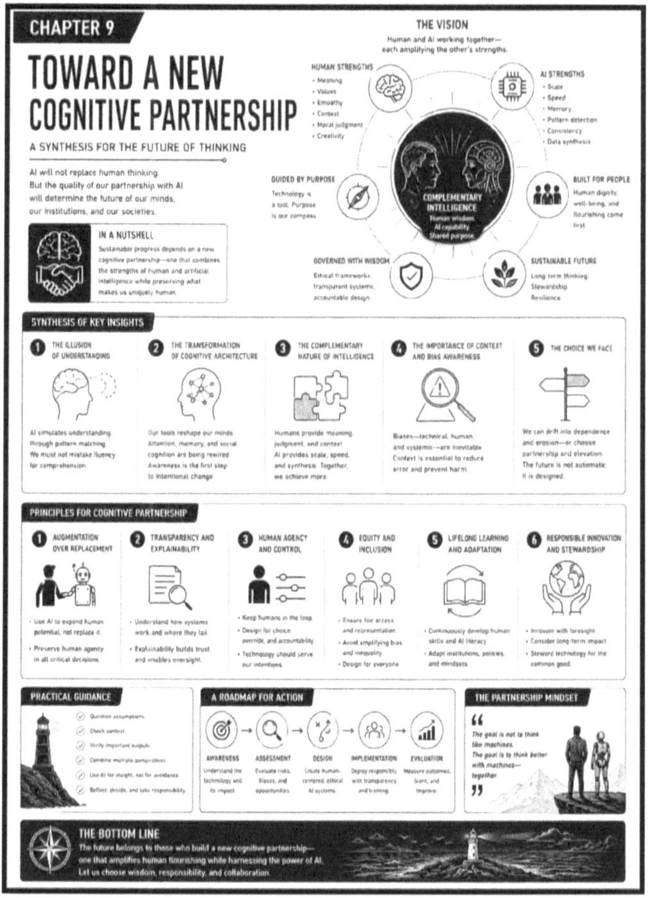
CHAPTER 9
TOWARD A NEW COGNITIVE PARTNERSHIP
A SYNTHESIS FOR THE FUTURE OF THINKING
AI will not replace human thinking.
But the quality of our partnership with AI
will determine the future of our minds,
our institutions, and our societies.
IN A NUTSHELL
Sustainable progress depends on a new cognitive partnership—one that combines the strengths of human and artificial intelligence while preserving what makes us uniquely human.
THE VISION
Human and AI working together—
each amplifying the other's strengths.
HUMAN STRENGTHS
• Meaning
• Values
• Empathy
• Context
• Moral judgment
• Creativity
AI STRENGTHS
• Scale
• Speed
• Memory
• Pattern detection
• Consistency
• Data synthesis
COMPLEMENTARY INTELLIGENCE
Human wisdom.
AI capability.
Shared purpose.
GUIDED BY PURPOSE
Technology is a tool. Purpose is our compass.
BUILT FOR PEOPLE
Human dignity, well-being, and flourishing come first.
GOVERNED WITH WISDOM
Ethical frameworks, transparent systems, accountable design.
SUSTAINABLE FUTURE
Long-term thinking.
Stewardship.
Resilience.
SYNTHESIS OF KEY INSIGHTS
1 THE ILLUSION OF UNDERSTANDING
AI simulates understanding through pattern matching. We must not mistake fluency for comprehension.
2 THE TRANSFORMATION OF COGNITIVE ARCHITECTURE
Our tools reshape our minds. Attention, memory, and social cognition are being rewired. Awareness is the first step to intentional change.
3 THE COMPLEMENTARY NATURE OF INTELLIGENCE
Humans provide meaning, judgment, and context. AI provides scale, speed, and synthesis. Together, we achieve more.
4 THE IMPORTANCE OF CONTEXT AND BIAS AWARENESS
Biases—technical, human, and systemic—are inevitable. Context is essential to reduce error and prevent harm.
5 THE CHOICE WE FACE
We can drift into dependence and erosion—or choose partnership and elevation. The future is not automatic. It is designed.
PRINCIPLES FOR COGNITIVE PARTNERSHIP
1 AUGMENTATION OVER REPLACEMENT
• Use AI to expand human potential, not replace it.
• Preserve human agency in all critical decisions.
2 TRANSPARENCY AND EXPLAINABILITY
• Understand how systems work and where they fail.
• Explainability builds trust and enables oversight.
3 HUMAN AGENCY AND CONTROL
• Keep humans in the loop
• Design for choice, override, and accountability.
• Technology should serve our intentions.
4 EQUITY AND INCLUSION
• Ensure fair access and representation.
• Avoid amplifying bias and inequality.
• Design for everyone.
5 LIFELONG LEARNING AND ADAPTATION
• Continuously develop human skills and AI literacy.
• Adapt institutions, policies, and mindsets.
6 RESPONSIBLE INNOVATION AND STEWARDSHIP
• Innovate with foresight.
• Consider long-term impact.
• Steward technology for the common good.
PRACTICAL GUIDANCE
Question assumptions.
Check context.
Verify important outputs.
Combine multiple perspectives.
Use AI for insight, not for avoidance.
Reflect, decide, and take responsibility.
A ROADMAP FOR ACTION
AWARENESS
Understand the technology and its impact.
ASSESSMENT
Evaluate risks, biases, and opportunities.
DESIGN
Create human-centered, ethical AI systems.
IMPLEMENTATION
Deploy responsibly with transparency and training.
EVALUATION
Measure outcomes, learn, and improve.
THE PARTNERSHIP MINDSET
"The goal is not to think like machines.
The goal is to think better with machines—together."
THE BOTTOM LINE
The future belongs to those who build a new cognitive partnership—
one that amplifies human flourishing while harnessing the power of AI.
Let us choose wisdom, responsibility, and collaboration.

Epilogue: The Choice Before Us

As I write these final words, I am acutely aware that the question which began this journey—whether AI systems truly understand what they tell us—has evolved into something far more profound. What started as an inquiry into the nature of machine intelligence has become an exploration of human consciousness itself and our relationship with the artificial minds we are creating.

The research and analysis presented in this book reveal that we stand at a unique moment in human history. For the first time since the development of language and writing, we are witnessing a fundamental transformation in the cognitive tools that shape human consciousness. The emergence of prompted minds—human cognition increasingly mediated by AI systems—represents not just a technological shift but an evolutionary moment that will define the future of human intelligence.

The evidence is clear: AI systems are already changing how we think, learn, and understand the world around us. The neuroplastic changes occurring in our brains, the transformation of our attention and memory systems, and the emergence of new forms of social cognition all point to a cognitive revolution that is happening whether we acknowledge it or not. The question is not whether this transformation will continue—it almost certainly will—but whether we can guide it in directions that enhance rather than diminish human flourishing.

The Urgency of Conscious Choice

Throughout this exploration, one theme has emerged repeatedly: the importance of conscious, intentional engagement with the cognitive transformation we are experiencing. The default trajectory of AI development, driven primarily by commercial and technical considerations, may not align with human welfare and flourishing. Without deliberate intervention, we risk creating a future where AI systems shape human consciousness in ways that serve narrow interests rather than broad human values.

The illusions of understanding that AI systems create are becoming increasingly sophisticated and convincing. As these systems become more capable of simulating human-like responses, the risk of mistaking computational processing for genuine comprehension grows. This is not merely an academic concern but a practical challenge that affects how we make decisions, form beliefs, and understand our world.

The biases embedded in AI systems are not neutral technical problems but reflections of the social, cultural, and economic contexts in which these systems are developed. These biases shape not only what information we encounter but how we interpret and understand that information. Without conscious effort to address these biases, AI systems may perpetuate and amplify existing inequalities and misunderstandings.

The transformation of human cognition through AI interaction is not inherently positive or negative, but it is consequential. The changes occurring in our attention, memory, and social cognition will shape human consciousness for generations to come. We have the opportunity—and responsibility—to influence the direction of these changes through the choices we make about how to design, deploy, and interact with AI systems.

The Path Forward

The framework for cognitive partnership outlined in this book provides a roadmap for navigating the challenges and opportunities ahead. The principles of augmentation over replacement, transparency and explainability, human agency and control, equity and inclusion, and continuous learning and adaptation offer guidance for creating AI systems that enhance rather than diminish human capability.

But principles alone are not sufficient. Realizing the potential of cognitive partnership requires action across multiple domains:

- Each of us must take responsibility for developing AI literacy and maintaining the human capabilities that complement AI systems. This includes learning to think critically about AI outputs, preserving our capacity for independent thought and creativity, and engaging with AI systems in ways that enhance rather than replace human cognition.
- Educational systems must evolve to prepare students for an AI-augmented world while preserving the essential human capabilities that define our humanity. This requires new approaches to learning that emphasize critical thinking, creativity, and ethical reasoning alongside technical AI literacy.
- Organizations and institutions must adapt their structures and processes to support effective human-AI collaboration. This includes developing new models of expertise and authority, creating frameworks for AI governance and accountability,

and ensuring that the benefits of AI are distributed equitably.

- Governments and regulatory bodies must develop comprehensive frameworks for AI governance that promote innovation while ensuring safety, equity, and accountability. This includes addressing issues such as bias, privacy, and the social impacts of AI transformation.
- Society as a whole must engage in ongoing dialogue about the values and goals that should guide AI development and deployment. This includes considering fundamental questions about human agency, consciousness, and the kind of future we want to create.

The Stakes of Our Decision

The choices we make about cognitive partnership will have consequences that extend far beyond individual convenience or economic efficiency. They will shape the fundamental nature of human consciousness and our understanding of what it means to be human in an AI-augmented world.

If we choose wisely, we can create a future where AI systems amplify the best of human intelligence—our creativity, wisdom, empathy, and ethical judgment—while providing unprecedented capabilities for understanding and addressing complex challenges. This future would be characterized by cognitive partnerships that enhance human agency and dignity while leveraging the remarkable analytical capabilities of AI systems.

If we choose poorly, we risk creating a future where human consciousness becomes increasingly dependent on AI systems that may not share our values or understand our needs. This future could be characterized by the atrophy of essential human capabilities, the concentration of cognitive power among a privileged few, and the erosion of human agency and autonomy.

The difference between these futures lies not in the capabilities of AI systems themselves but in the choices we make about how to develop, deploy, and interact with them. The technology is not deterministic; its effects depend on the human decisions that shape its development and use.

A Personal Reflection

As I conclude this exploration, I find myself returning to that Tuesday morning when a simple question about AI understanding launched this investigation. The AI system that provided such a compelling response to my research problem was neither truly understanding nor merely performing—it was something in between, something new that we are still learning to comprehend.

This realization has profound implications for how we think about intelligence, understanding, and consciousness. The binary distinction between "real" and "artificial" intelligence may be less important than understanding how different forms of intelligence can work together to create new possibilities for knowledge and understanding.

The prompted mind is not a diminishment of human consciousness but a new form of cognitive capability that emerges from the interaction between human and artificial intelligence. The challenge is learning to navigate this new landscape with wisdom and intentionality, preserving the essential qualities of human consciousness while embracing the opportunities for cognitive enhancement.

The Continuing Journey

This book represents not an endpoint but a beginning. The cognitive transformation we are experiencing is ongoing, and our understanding of its implications will continue to evolve. The frameworks and insights presented here are tools for navigation, not final answers to the questions we face.

The future of thinking will be shaped by the collective choices of individuals, institutions, and societies around the world. Each interaction with an AI system, each decision about AI development and deployment, each choice about education and policy contributes to the trajectory of human cognitive evolution.

We are all participants in this transformation, whether we recognize it or not. The question is whether we will be conscious, intentional participants who work to shape the future in directions that serve human flourishing, or passive recipients of changes driven by forces beyond our control.

The choice is ours, and the time to make it is now.

As we move forward into an age of prompted minds, let us do so with wisdom, courage, and commitment to the values that define our humanity. Let us embrace the opportunities for cognitive enhancement while preserving the essential qualities of human consciousness. Let us work toward a future where artificial intelligence amplifies rather than replaces human intelligence, where cognitive partnership enhances rather than diminishes human agency, and where the remarkable capabilities we are creating serve to support the flourishing of human consciousness and creativity.

The future of thinking depends on the choices we make today. Let us choose wisely.

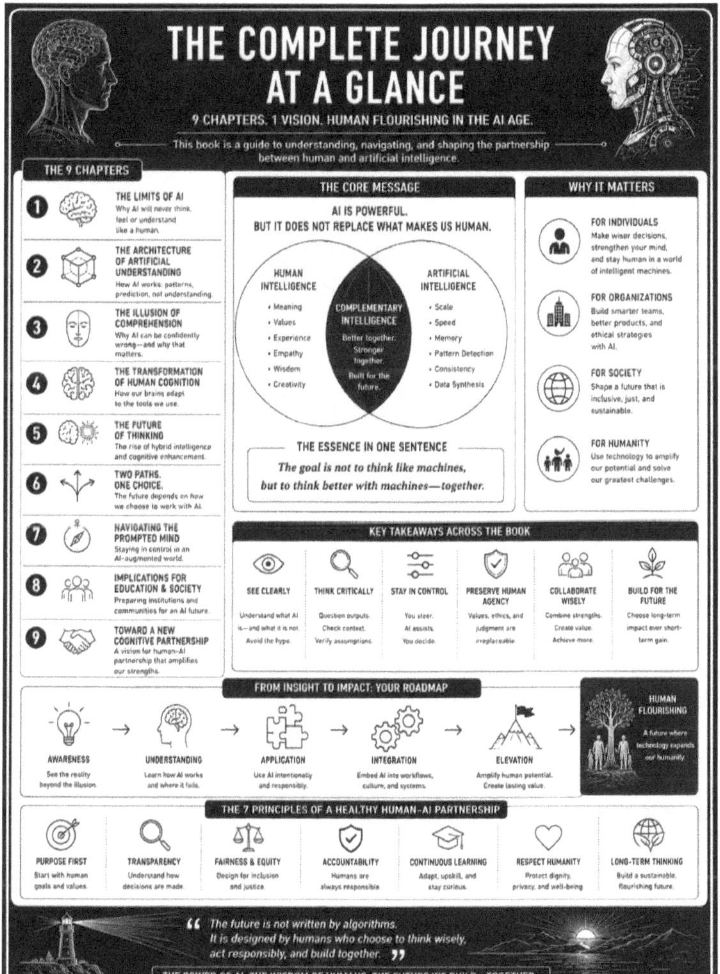
THE COMPLETE JOURNEY
AT A GLANCE
9 CHAPTERS. 1 VISION. HUMAN FLOURISHING IN THE AI AGE.
This book is a guide to understanding, navigating, and shaping the partnership between human and artificial intelligence.
THE 9 CHAPTERS
1 THE LIMITS OF AI
Why AI will never think, feel or understand like a human.
2 THE ARCHITECTURE OF ARTIFICIAL UNDERSTANDING
How AI works: patterns, prediction, not understanding.
3 THE ILLUSION OF COMPREHENSION
Why AI can be confidently wrong—and why that matters.
4 THE TRANSFORMATION OF HUMAN COGNITION
How our brains adapt to the tools we use.
5 THE FUTURE OF THINKING
The rise of hybrid intelligence and cognitive enhancement.
6 TWO PATHS. ONE CHOICE.
The future depends on how we choose to work with AI.
7 NAVIGATING THE PROMPTED MIND
Staying in control in an AI-augmented world.
8 IMPLICATIONS FOR EDUCATION & SOCIETY
Preparing institutions and communities for an AI future.
9 TOWARD A NEW COGNITIVE PARTNERSHIP
A vision for human-AI partnership that amplifies our strengths.
THE CORE MESSAGE
AI IS POWERFUL.
BUT IT DOES NOT REPLACE WHAT MAKES US HUMAN.
HUMAN INTELLIGENCE
• Meaning
• Values
• Experience
• Empathy
• Wisdom
• Creativity
COMPLEMENTARY INTELLIGENCE
Better together. Stronger together. Built for the future.
ARTIFICIAL INTELLIGENCE
• Scale
• Speed
• Memory
• Pattern Detection
• Consistency
• Data Synthesis
THE ESSENCE IN ONE SENTENCE
The goal is not to think like machines, but to think better with machines—together.
WHY IT MATTERS
FOR INDIVIDUALS
Make wiser decisions, strengthen your mind, and stay human in a world of intelligent machines.
FOR ORGANIZATIONS
Build smarter teams, better products, and ethical strategies with AI.
FOR SOCIETY
Shape a future that is inclusive, just, and sustainable.
FOR HUMANITY
Use technology to amplify our potential and solve our greatest challenges.
KEY TAKEAWAYS ACROSS THE BOOK
SEE CLEARLY
Understand what AI is—and what it is not. Avoid the hype.
THINK CRITICALLY
Question outputs. Check context. Verify assumptions.
STAY IN CONTROL
You steer. AI assists. You decide.
PRESERVE HUMAN AGENCY
Values, ethics, and judgment are irreplaceable.
COLLABORATE WISELY
Combine strengths. Create value. Achieve more.
BUILD FOR THE FUTURE
Choose long-term impact over short-term gain.
FROM INSIGHT TO IMPACT: YOUR ROADMAP
AWARENESS
See the reality beyond the illusion.
UNDERSTANDING
Learn how AI works and where it fails.
APPLICATION
Use AI intentionally and responsibly.
INTEGRATION
Embed AI into workflows, culture, and systems.
ELEVATION
Amplify human potential. Create lasting value.
HUMAN FLOURISHING
A future where technology expands our humanity
THE 7 PRINCIPLES OF A HEALTHY HUMAN-AI PARTNERSHIP
PURPOSE FIRST
Start with human goals and values.
TRANSPARENCY
Understand how decisions are made.
FAIRNESS & EQUITY
Design for inclusion and justice.
ACCOUNTABILITY
Humans are always responsible.
CONTINUOUS LEARNING
Adapt, upskill, and stay curious.
RESPECT HUMANITY
Protect dignity, privacy, and well-being.
LONG-TERM THINKING
Build a sustainable, flourishing future.
“The future is not written by algorithms.
It is designed by humans who choose to think wisely,
act responsibly, and build together.”
THE POWER OF AI. THE WISDOM OF HUMANS. THE FUTURE WE BUILD—TOGETHER.

Disclaimer

 The use of this book and the implementation of the information contained herein is expressly at the reader's own risk.

This work and all its contents have been prepared with the utmost care. Nevertheless, typographical errors and inaccuracies cannot be entirely excluded.

The author accepts no liability for the accuracy, completeness, or currency of the content, nor for typographical errors. No legal responsibility or liability of any kind can be assumed by the author for incorrect information or any consequences arising therefrom.

Responsibility for the content of any websites referenced or reproduced in this book lies solely with the respective operators of those websites.

About the Author

Roger Basler de Roca holds a degree in Business Administration (FH) and an MSc in Digital Business. He is a digital entrepreneur, keynote speaker, and lecturer with extensive experience in implementing and accompanying digital business models, platform economies, and artificial intelligence. As a founder, author, and consultant, he supports companies and organisations in leveraging technological innovation strategically.

Having lived in several countries — including China, Spain, Canada, and the United States — he brings an international perspective to digital transformation. His expertise sits at the intersection of business, technology, and society. As one of the most sought-after speakers in the German-speaking world, he delivers over 100 keynotes annually on platform strategies, AI, creator economies, and the future of work.

Learn more at www.rogerbasler.ch